MW00397917

GOOD
IS THE
NEW
COOL
GUIDE TO

PERSONAL
PURPOSE

GOOD IS THE NEW COOL GUIDE TO

PERSONAL PURPOSE

DESIGNING A MEANINGFUL AND PROSPEROUS CAREER

AFDHEL AZIZ & BOBBY JONES

WILEY

Published by John Wiley & Sons, Inc., Hoboken, New Jersey.
Published simultaneously in Canada.

For general information on our other products and services or for technical support, please contact our Customer Care Department within the United States at (800) 762-2974, outside the United States at (317) 572-3993 or fax (317) 572-4002.

Wiley also publishes its books in a variety of electronic formats. Some content that appears in print may not be available in electronic formats. For more information about Wiley products, visit our web site at www.wiley.com.

Library of Congress Cataloging-in-Publication Data
Names: Aziz, Afdhel (Branding professional), author. | Jones, Bobby
   (Marketing professional), author.
Title: Good is the new cool guide to personal purpose : designing a
   meaningful and prosperous career / Afdhel Aziz, Bobby Jones.
Description: Hoboken, New Jersey : Wiley, [2025] | Includes index.
Identifiers: LCCN 2024023827 (print) | LCCN 2024023828 (ebook) | ISBN
   9781394274864 (hardback) | ISBN 9781394274888 (adobe pdf) | ISBN
   9781394274871 (epub)
Subjects: LCSH: Career development. | Self-actualization (Psychology)
Classification: LCC HF5381 .A95 2025 (print) | LCC HF5381 (ebook) | DDC
   650.1–dc23/eng/20240628
LC record available at https://lccn.loc.gov/2024023827
LC ebook record available at https://lccn.loc.gov/2024023828

Cover Design: Wiley

This book is dedicated to our parents, Vada and Bob Jones, and Fathima and Shibly Aziz, who showed us what a life of service can be.

CONTENTS

INTRODUCTION

T he house lights dim. The smoke machines billow out clouds of theatrical fog. And then rising from the stage on a podium appears the figure of Kanye West—or Ye, as he is currently known—his hands thrown up as the throbbing beat of his song "Flashing Lights" starts. He's wearing all black with massive gold chains hanging around his neck. He sings:

She don't believe in shooting stars
But she believes in shoes and cars

Around us are a thousand influencers and guests who have been invited to this "secret" show in Brooklyn, courtesy of the brand we have been working for the past few years—Afdhel on the client side, Bobby leading one of the agencies who helped put this whole show together.

It should be a moment of triumph, a shining high point for a music platform that we have spent years developing, which celebrates the best of hip hop. This moment has seen us work with some of the biggest names in music over the years—Ludacris, Big Boi from Outkast, Nas, Rick Ross, and so many more.

Instead, what we see is this: everyone in the building is looking at their phones, posting the moment to social media, broadcasting their status to the world—look at me, look at my access. They are not actually paying attention to the performance happening on stage. Instead they are too busy reflecting the moment off their shiny egos.

The moment felt hollow.

After 20 years of doing this—using our Passion for pop culture to help create experiences and content for some of the biggest brands in the world—the work didn't give us meaning anymore, didn't give us the same joy, the same satisfaction.

You know that moment in the Roadrunner cartoons when Wiley E. Coyote runs off a cliff and doesn't realize it? While his legs keep moving, but there's nothing underneath him?

That was that moment for us.

When the cool stopped being cool.

BOBBY

remember when I held my son, Miles, for the first time. His big brown eyes peered up at me from beneath his beautiful curly hair, awakening a sense of love so intense it was as though my heart had shifted shape.

I whispered a promise to him in that moment, a solemn vow that I would always, unequivocally, be the best father I could be. But the relentless grind of work, the voracious beast that it is, began to test my promise even when Miles was just a small child.

There was one particular day that's forever in my memory. The norm of my work-life balance had tilted over, dangerously skewed toward work. My agency client, an increasingly demanding brand, was calling constantly.

Evening calls turned into late-night discussions, bleeding into early morning updates, and they peppered my weekends with insistent inquiries about things that, in the rearview mirror of time, weren't important.

The day that stands out in my mind was a late evening, heavy with the humidity of a New York summer. I was returning from a long day at work, just stepping off the train when my street corner came into view. The ring from my phone disrupted my wandering mind in a way that was all too familiar. It was my client, with their normal, demanding tone.

The moment I picked up, before a hello could part from my lips, I was hit with a barrage of questions.

A crisis was unfolding in their company, and they sounded desperate, helpless. It felt like being swept up in a tumultuous sea of requests, each one demanding immediate attention.

As I waded through my client's words, I turned the corner of my street. With the phone still glued to my ear, a small figure distant on the sidewalk caught my eye—my son, Miles, now three years old with his tiny hand wrapped securely in my wife Renee's grasp. I caught his eyes, and it was as though the world exhaled.

His face lit up with a wide grin and, like a rocket, he shot off, barreling toward me.

He was running with the eagerness of a child who can't wait to see his dad. As he covered the distance between us, the client's voice in my ear was a sharp contrast, drawing me back into her whirlpool of problems. Miles ran toward me, each step with pure joy. But, as he got close enough to jump into my arms, he stumbled and fell.

His hands slapped the ground, followed quickly by the side of his face. The hurt was immediate, his tears, a torrent. I could see his small body curled on the ground, an image that hurt my heart. My client's voice, which had been a steady drone, suddenly seemed to grow louder with distress.

On instinct, I hit mute on the phone and raced to my son's side.

I fell to my knees, not caring about the hard concrete. All that mattered was the tiny boy in front of me. I held him close, making sure he was okay, providing the big comforting hug he'd just been running toward.

Cradling Miles in one arm, the phone still gripped in the other, my client's muffled voice broke through, "Hey, are you still there?" It was in that split second that I realized the stark contrast of the things I held. One was the life I was devoted to, the other, an obligation that increasingly lacked importance. Yet the pull of my work, strangely, didn't go away.

That moment was a wake-up call.

It was clear that if I was to become the father I had committed myself to be, I could not continue to blur the boundaries between work and family, holding them both with equal weight. It was vital, an undeniable truth, that my life must reflect a commitment to prioritizing my family first, not merely as a concept but in my daily actions, decisions, and interactions.

It was in that conflicting moment, cradling Miles in one arm and balancing work in the other, that a decision became clear within me. I vowed to ensure that Miles would always take precedence, that my attention to him and my family would not be betrayed by unimportant work calls or crisis management.

Shortly thereafter, a slow but profound transformation began to happen in my life. A new way of being began to take shape, one aligned with my core values, my highest priorities, and the promises I had made to myself and the ones I loved.

If circumstances ever required me to be away from my family for work, I pledged to myself that the work I did had to be meaningful, impactful, and purposeful. It had to be a contribution that felt aligned with my deepest convictions and was worthy of the time spent away from those I held closest.

As I recount this story, it is with a deep sense of gratitude.

The incident served as a necessary wake-up call that helped me redefine my priorities. Now, whenever I find myself juggling between work and family, I remember the feel of Miles's small frame in my arms and the urgency in my client's voice.

It serves as a powerful reminder of the promise I made to myself and to my son that day, a promise I am determined to keep.

AFDHEL

The next week, I had to go on a business trip again, this time a long one. I would be away for a week.

At this stage, I was living in Cobble Hill, Brooklyn, with my wife Rukshana and our son Nuri, who was three years old at the time.

We had adopted Nuri when he was one year old from Sri Lanka. His brave birth mother spent a year living in my parents' house in Sri Lanka looking after him until we were able to finalize all the paperwork to bring him into the United States.

Then one day she handed him to us, and we got on a plane, and he left the country of his birth to move into our small two-bedroom apartment.

The trauma of separation from his birth mother was severe. Every night, for six months, he would cry for hours, scared and fearful of suddenly being in this new place where everything was different from the warm, tropical home where he spent the first year of his life.

We would spend hours holding him, calming him down, making him feel safe and loved and cared for. We would look out of the window at the falling snow, marveling at the world blanketed in white.

Over time Nuri began to slowly acclimatize to his new home. He began to trust us and feel safe.

But he still hated it when I went away to work. He was too young to understand that was part of what I had to do—to travel around the country, to travel around the world, all in service of my job.

That particular trip, he said something to me as I went out of the door after kissing and hugging him.

He said, "See you next week, Dada."

I couldn't stop thinking about what he said on that entire business trip. In the taxi, in the airport, on the plane, checking into another anonymous hotel.

"See you next week, Dada."

It kept burning me up inside.

A week was a long time in the life of a three-year-old.

When I got back home, I couldn't wait to spend time with him. I hugged and kissed him, and we decided to go and spend some father-son time together in one of our favorite places—the little park around the corner from our house.

After he played for a bit, we sat on the bench, overlooking the playground, and talked. He told me about everything he had been doing in his kindergarten class, all the new things he had learned.

I said to him, "Hey, I'm really sorry I had to go away for such a long time on this trip. You know, I had to go to work."

And he looked at me with his beautiful eyes and said, "It's okay, Dada. I know your work is important."

And then he paused and said to me, "So . . . what is your work?"

At that point, something snapped inside of me.

I didn't have the heart to tell this little boy that my work was about selling more stuff.

That I had missed a week of his life because I needed to do something that had become increasingly meaningless to me.

I started to think about the role model I was setting for him, as a father.

I started to think about the world I was helping create for him and his generation to inherit and whether my work was making it any better.

My eyes welled up with tears.

I was overwhelmed by the moment.

All I could do was give him a big hug.

Something inside of me had changed.

I knew that I couldn't go on doing this work.

But I still had no idea what I could do next.

But little did I know that someone who I had grown to trust and admire was going through the exact same thing, that journey of self-examination and doubt.

AFDHEL AND BOBBY

Ping!

The email arrived, the subject line reading, "Let's grab lunch." We decided on an Italian restaurant in Chelsea, Manhattan's art district. It was winter in New York, making the idea of a warm bowl of pasta appealing. We hadn't seen each other for some time. We had both taken a needed break after an eventful year of music projects—from electrifying New York nights spent with Alicia Keys to the pulsating vibrancy of California's Coachella. It seemed the right time to reconnect. We greeted each other outside with handshakes and hugs, and as we like to say, "It was all love."

We walked in with the tantalizing aroma of garlic and tomatoes wafting through the air, offering the perfect warm welcome. The maître d' guided us to our table. As we broke bread, the conversation started with a standard "How are you doing?" But a deeper question soon followed: "How are you doing, really?" The initial response was the usual positive and somewhat superficial assurance. But with the second question, the mood shifted. We both leaned back, exhaled, and knew this wouldn't be an ordinary lunch.

Over the course of two hours, we enjoyed our appetizers, pasta, and drinks. The pasta had been so good that Bobby ordered it twice, giving rise to what we now call "Bobby Jones'ing" a meal.

We shared our collective guilt at feeling that we were not being the fathers that we wanted to be with our sons. We were vulnerable with each other about the fact that we not only felt that we were not being good role models to them—but that we didn't feel that our work was leaving a better world for them to inherit.

Over the next two hours, we found ourselves diving into the depths of what it truly meant to be a marketer in that moment. We wondered if our legacy would be limited to just getting more people to buy more things. There was a shared sense of dissatisfaction and a desire for more meaningful, significant work.

We recalled a slogan we'd seen, "Good is the new cool." It was a poster on the subway that one of us had seen as the train pulled out of the station, written by some unknown copywriter for a product. It had seemed like a message from the universe.

We found it resonated with us in an inspiring way.

Could we change the way we worked and lived to better align with this idea? We didn't know, but the idea of writing a book began to form. It could guide us and others like us seeking to find Purpose in our work in a cool, profitable, and meaningful way. It was clear we were both hungry for something much more than our meals could satisfy.

By the time we finished lunch, we had made a decision. We were ready to embark on a journey of discovery, toward a future we weren't quite sure was possible. Leaving the restaurant that day, the wintry air felt a little less biting, our spirits lifted by our hopeful conversation. We were no longer just two marketers looking for the next successful campaign, but adventurers on a mission to infuse our professional lives with greater meaning. Over the next few weeks, our conversation that day became the seed of many discussions, emails, and brainstorming sessions. We found ourselves delving into uncharted territories, questioning the status quo, and daring to imagine a world where business was not just about making profits but also making a positive impact. It was the beginning.

Our lunches at the Italian restaurant in Chelsea became more frequent. But they were no longer just about enjoying the pasta, although we did 'Bobby Jones' a meal a few more times! These gatherings became our touch points, spaces where we could share our insights, voice our concerns, and keep each other accountable to the journey we had embarked on.

By the time the New York winter thawed into spring, we had a new-found sense of excitement about our work. We were no longer on a quest for more profits; we were on a quest for more Purpose. And we had a feeling that this was just the beginning.

We didn't know it at the time, but what we were experiencing was what we would later call a "moment of clarity"—when we knew that we had to stop doing what we were doing in life, but we didn't know what we were supposed to do next. As we'd come to find out, this would be a common moment in everyone's quest to find Purpose in their lives.

PART I

OUR PURPOSE JOURNEY (INSPIRATION)

This first section of the book is a narrative of our journey to find our Purpose in the middle of our careers. The goal is to inspire you, through our own stories and transformations, to go on your own journey. If we can do it, anyone can do it.

CHAPTER 1

THE CALL
TO ADVENTURE

> There is no road, the road is made by walking.
> —Antonio Machado, Spanish poet

As 2011 began, we were set in motion with nothing more than a title, *Good Is the New Cool*. What began as a vague notion quickly morphed into vivid imagination and an intention in our hearts to help ourselves and others find greater meaning and Purpose in their work. We thought about the kind of book that would inspire us as readers and the transformation it could catalyze within us. As we shared our concept with our colleagues, the idea resonated deeply with many who shared our desire for more fulfillment in our work; we were not alone in this quest.

During this early stage, we were still immersed in our day jobs, which started to feel like an ordinary backdrop against the vibrant dreamscape we were painting. Afdhel's tiny Brooklyn apartment morphed into an impromptu studio for our budding masterpiece.

We would pace up and down the small hallway between the bedroom and the kitchen, a photograph of Muhammad Ali gracefully standing at the bottom of a Miami swimming pool watching over us—a daily inspiration of how courage and imagination could create a life worth living.

THE JOURNEY OF WRITING OUR FIRST BOOK

As we wrote down every idea that popped into our heads, that corridor transformed into an avalanche of sticky notes, with quotes, dreams, and half-baked ideas scribbled on every inch of the walls.

Our spirits were alive with the limitless possibilities that lay before us. We wanted to learn from everyone who seemed to have found the path we were searching for. We turned into amateur journalists, actively seeking out people to interview.

But as we began the next step in our journey, deep-rooted doubts and fears began to emerge. Imposter syndrome gnawed at us. Would people we wanted to talk with say, "Who in the hell are you?" The weight of these insecurities was overwhelming, but our core mission—to empower people with a renewed sense of Purpose— anchored us.

We faithfully moved forward, and good fortune kicked in. One phone call led to another, and we were soon globe-trotting, networking, and delving deep into a plethora of stories. Bevy Smith introduced us to Mimi Valdes—an awe-inspiring creator working on an upcoming moving script titled *Hidden Figures*. Another friend introduced us to Jaha Johnson, whose near-death experience in a surfing accident inspired his work with music artists such as Common, Usher, and Mary J Blige, with Purpose and dedication.

Our relationships in the music business gave us access to music managers such as Scooter Braun and Bobby Campbell, who shared how they advised their megastar clients such as Justin Bieber and Lady Gaga to create with Purpose.

We looked at companies such as TOM's, Patagonia, and The Honest Company, which were creating a new paradigm for business, where doing good and doing well were in harmony.

We researched an inspiring wave of nonprofits such as Global Citizen, Pencils of Promise, and Charity Water, which were innovating in the space through bold use of culture and technology.

We felt as if we were investigative reporters, starting to see the shape of a new movement, a new shift in the zeitgeist of the world, toward a more values-driven approach, something that rejected the shallowness of society in favor of something deeper, where "good" in fact was becoming "cool," just like that poster on the subway had said.

Four years we labored, without deadlines, allowing our work to mature organically. We had a finished manuscript but no idea what to do with it.

Here came the doubts again. Would anyone read our book? How would we get it out in the world? Would our book languish in obscurity?

THE PHONE CALL THAT CHANGED EVERYTHING

I'll never forget the moment when our lives changed forever. I was in the back of a taxicab going down one of San Francisco's famous sweeping hills when my phone rang with an unfamiliar number.

"Hello, I read your book and would like to represent you as an agent."

I remember frantically trying to listen to the call while simultaneously googling who this person was. I remember staring at the screen at the agent's profile on their company website and all the famous authors he represented.

No way was this happening. No way was this person offering to represent us. Was I being punked by one of my friends? It usually took years to find an agent. But thanks to a kind and gracious friend who introduced us, we got there much faster.

The universe has a wonderful way of showing you the next path on your journey.

A week later, we signed a contract to find us a publisher.

The agent returned with bittersweet news; out of 19 publishers, 18 declined. However, one—Regan Arts—accepted.

The Regan Arts office in Soho was a breath of fresh air, a vibrant nexus of youthful energy and genuine excitement for our work. It buzzed with life as young editors huddled over manuscripts, the scent of freshly brewed coffee wafting through the room. There was an electric undercurrent, a sense of determination and an unshakeable Passion for the power of literature. Conversations swirled around the latest literary sensation, innovative marketing strategies, and the delicate art of author-publisher relationships. The atmosphere in the office was not just invigorating but genuinely inspiring, an opportunity to bring our idea to life.

One of the posters on the wall had a quote from Kenneth Rexroth, "Against the ruin of the world, there is only one defense—the creative act." Those words perfectly captured the spirit of our intention. It was a sign; this was the place where our creative act would find its wings.

"AGAINST THE RUIN OF THE WORLD, THERE IS ONLY ONE DEFENSE—THE CREATIVE ACT."

—Kenneth Rexroth

An avalanche of activities ensued for the next ten months—interviews, writing, rewriting, editing, cover designing, PR meetings, and distribution discussions. Each day brought a new wave of excitement, a potent mix of exhilaration and exhaustion. The feeling was like riding a runaway train, powered by ambition and steered by Purpose.

The day came for us to see the cover design for the first time, a milestone moment that we'll never forget. Our bright orange cover, pulsating with energy and promise, stood out from the pack. It was emboldened with typography that was at once brash and elegant, making an indelible impression. It was a signal of optimism and hope, a tangible symbol of the work we had poured our hearts and souls into, and a declaration of the change we wanted to create.

In October 2016, we received our first copies of our book *Good Is the New Cool: Market Like You Give a Damn* (what is today known as *Good Is the New Cool Guide to Meaningful Marketing: How Brands Can Win with Conscious Consumers*).

It was a physical expression of our shared dreams and years of hard work. The moments of unveiling were made all the more special by sharing them with our families, who had been our unwavering pillars of support throughout the journey.

Holding the book in our hands, we could feel the weight of our triumph. The pages held the imprint of countless hours spent huddled over keyboards, the all-day brainstorming sessions fueled by delivery food and determination, and the oscillating waves of doubt and faith. Each word was a testament to our relentless pursuit of impact, each chapter an articulation of our shared vision and individual growth.

We celebrated this moment, over four years in the making, with a mixture of elation and relief. Our faces reflected the glow of accomplishment, our eyes sparkled with the joy of creation. We had transformed our vision into a reality, etching our thoughts and experiences into the archives of literary history.

We had no idea of what was to come, of the myriad experiences, both daunting and exhilarating, that lay ahead of us. Yet, at that moment, none of that mattered. We stood on the precipice of the unknown, emboldened by the sense of achievement and the pride in our work. Regardless of the path that lay ahead, we had created something that we were immensely proud of, a symbol of our collective creativity and resilience.

THE DAY THE BOOK CAME OUT

The release day had finally arrived! We couldn't believe this day was here. We woke up excited with anticipation, like a young child on Christmas morning.

It was an autumn morning as we walked down our neighborhood Brooklyn Street. The streets were bustling with people getting their morning coffees. The sky was clear, bright blue, marking the end of the golden hues of sunrise and the arrival of full daylight. The bookstores were starting to open, and we were first to walk inside.

Our hearts were pounding like tribal drums. Shaking with anticipation we just said, "Can you believe this day is finally here?"

It was like stepping into a dream that we've had a thousand times, only to find that it is real.

As we pushed open the door, the smell of new books greeted us, one of the best smells in the world. We walked through the aisles, and there, under a soft halo of light, was our book. The cover, vibrant orange and full of promise, winked at us as if acknowledging the long journey we'd undertaken together.

Afdhel picked up a copy, his fingers caressing the pages he knew so well, and he felt an outpouring of emotions. It's as if every word was a piece of his soul, and now it was here, tangible and ready to embrace the world.

Bobby stood next to him, with a copy in his hand, an unspoken kinship in this moment. We had both poured our deepest beliefs, our sleepless nights, and our boundless hopes into those pages.

Seeing your book on the shelf of a bookstore for the first time is like listening to the radio and hearing your song come on—it's a feeling of pride and joy that lights up your entire body with joy.

A woman nearby picked up a copy and started leafing through it. Bobby's heart skipped a beat. This was it—the connection we had yearned for. Our words, our vision was now an extended hand reaching out to those searching for a spark.

With that, we felt the gravity of what we had accomplished. This book was more than paper and ink; it was a light, the beginning of a movement, and truly the essence of who we are.

Our minds were a whirlwind, but amid this storm, we found calmness and pride. We had not just written a book; we had sowed our own seeds of change.

As we stepped out of the bookstore, the city around us felt different—as if it had been touched by our work. We looked at each other, nodded, and realized that our journey had only just begun.

LAUNCHING THE BOOK INTO THE WORLD

As days turned into weeks, and weeks into months, we found ourselves diving into a whirlwind of events and new experiences. Book signings, speaking engagements, interviews, and podcast appearances became a part of our routine. The reception of *Good Is the New Cool Guide to Meaningful Marketing* was overwhelmingly positive, and we felt fulfilled that our message was reaching people in meaningful ways.

We had the opportunity to connect with countless individuals who shared their stories and how our book had inspired them. This connection with our readers was, undoubtedly, one of the most rewarding parts of this journey.

Looking back, the inception of *Good Is the New Cool Guide to Meaningful Marketing* was more than just the creation of a book; it was the beginning of a movement. It was a testament that with Passion, persistence, and a bit of luck, individuals can make a positive impact in the world.

Today our journey continues, as we constantly seek new stories, insights, and opportunities to create meaningful change. We remain grounded and committed to the belief that "good" can indeed be the new "cool" and that through creativity and collaboration, we can all contribute to a better world.

CHAPTER 2

FINDING OUR PURPOSE

Your real job in life is to figure out what it is you are called to do.
—Oprah Winfrey

We experienced an amazing journey while writing and promoting the book. One of the most inspiring aspects of that journey was meeting countless people who had found a sense of Purpose in what they were doing. They found meaning in it and connected their work with values that they held dear. They discovered a clear why that informed their creativity and actions.

As we wrote about everyone else's work and Purpose, it began to dawn on us that we had never actually gone on the journey to discover our own. This realization became even clearer, and the hunger to discover Purpose in our own lives and work grew increasingly important to us.

WHAT WAS OUR PURPOSE? AND HOW WOULD WE BRING IT TO LIFE?

We realized that we needed to embark on new journeys, not ones focused on the Purposes of others but a journey to discover our own why and reason for being. This was not an easy task and neither of us has a clue where to start our journey.

In many ways, that experience is what makes the struggle to understand our Purpose so relatable and understandable. We knew that Purpose was our destination and were clear on our starting point, but we had no way of understanding the path from where we were to where we wanted to go. We needed a guide, a sense of direction—in essence, we needed a GPS.

It turned out that the person who could give us that direction was someone who had been right there in Bobby's life all along. His own journey to finding his Purpose could not have been more dramatic in its own right.

INTRODUCING TRU PETTIGREW

South Beach, Miami.

On a November night, the air was alight with excitement. The Versace Mansion, renowned for hosting some of the most illustrious and extravagant events in culture, was buzzing with anticipation. This historical venue had been home to luminaries, fashion icons, music legends, artistic geniuses, and cultural creators. It was a place where people had gathered for decades to celebrate life in the most opulent and fabulous ways, and tonight 400 of us were there to continue that tradition.

We were attending the birthday celebration of Tru Pettigrew, the marketing maven. The speakers blared the beat of the hottest songs of the year and an eclectic mix of classics, making sure the energy never waned.

Dressed to the nines, the 400 guests exuded glamor. The women swayed elegantly to the beat, dressed in the most fashionable couture. The men, donning tuxedos and their finest clothes, danced the night away, not minding the sweat that soaked through their garments.

The party was outdoors, and hundreds of people had traveled from across the country and around the world to celebrate Pettigrew's birthday. And as the music softened, it became clear that there was going to be a moment that demanded everyone's attention. As the DJ dimmed the sound, people's gaze shifted upward, trying to see where the focus should be directed. A spotlight shone on a doorway at the top of a staircase, and rhythmic hip-hop beats began to fill up the night air.

Emerging from the doorway was none other than Tru Pettigrew, clad in an impeccably tailored Armani black suit, a crisp white shirt, and a perfectly knotted black tie. Black sunglasses shielded his eyes from the spotlight's glare and the adoring gazes of the crowd.

As the music resumed, it became evident that this was Tru's moment, and he was living it to the fullest. With each step down the staircase, he savored the feeling, his smile radiating pure joy.

Once Tru reached the ground level, standing among the guests, from the gaze of the crowd, he appeared to be elevated even further. He lifted his hands as if embracing the night sky, basking in the moment.

This night was, in many ways, the culmination of a lifetime of hard work. Tru Pettigrew had established himself as one of the most respected and recognized marketers in the industry.

But as we looked at Tru reveling in what seemed like the pinnacle of his career, none of us knew there was an undertone of deep dissatisfaction within him.

Many years later, he told us the story of overhearing someone at that party describing him excitedly on the phone.

"Yeah, I'm at Tru's party! You know the guy with the Armani suits and the Rolex watches?"

He realized that he was being described not in terms of his unique qualities as a human being—his innate kindness and wisdom, his humor and soul—but in terms of his consumption and materialism.

It was a moment that shook him at his core.

Little did we know it, but that night was the beginning of a journey. He was about to embark on a search to fill a void that no spotlight could satiate.

HOW BOBBY MET TRU

In the early 2000s, my friends and business partners Kenny Mac, Tony Fair, and Kirk Taylor and I decided to move to NYC together. NYC was where dreams came to life, and we had big ones in store.

Tony offered to drive us to New York, but I needed some cash to start with, and I had none. My parents had a tin, the kind you would normally use for holiday cookies, Christmas cookies to be precise. They used it to store loose change, particularly quarters. Over the years, they filled multiple tins with quarters. As Tony waited for me downstairs in the car, I swiftly stuffed all my clothes and belongings into trash bags. Tony helped me load them into the car, and then I rushed upstairs to my parents' room. I opened one of the tins and poured as many quarters as I could into a Ziploc bag. With my makeshift fortune secured, I hopped into the car, and we set off for New York to start a new life.

We arrived in New York in June of 2002, a day bustling with the Puerto Rican Day Parade. We had started a marketing company, Direct Impulse, and had moved to the city with dreams of dominating the industry. The first year was, to say the least, a challenge.

Our first night in New York was spent in our small one-bedroom apartment, where we began to strategize our plan of action. We needed money, and one thing we had a reputation for was throwing amazing parties. So we shifted our focus toward what we did best at the time—organizing events. We went downtown and met a promoter named Chris Reda. Together, we planned a party at a Midtown restaurant named Guastavino's. Hosted on Fridays, it quickly gained popularity and soon hosted stars such as Jay-Z, Beyoncé, Jennifer Lopez, and Fat Joe, along with athletes from the Yankees and the Knicks, and other celebrities and supermodels.

Among our team of promoters was Eric Soler, a charismatic Puerto Rican born and raised in New York. He was the kind of guy everybody wanted to be around—hilarious, cool, and an expert in creating an unforgettable time. The parties were resounding successes, but not everything was rosy.

As summer cooled down, shifting to fall, the foundation in my life began to break apart like leaves from autumn branches. During this time, my father was diagnosed with terminal cancer. My world crumbled as I spent the next six months caring for him. My father's health slowly eroded, and in the whirlwind of grief and struggle, I was also facing the reality that we were running out of money and options for our company. Then, a chance call from Soler turned things around for us.

Eric introduced us to an accomplished marketing executive who was looking to partner with connected, young entrepreneurs. For months, as I was caring for my father, I spoke with this executive over the phone, learning about his vision for the company.

After my father's passing, I knew it was time to give this partnership a shot. We agreed to meet at the Hyatt Grand. I dressed in a crisp white shirt and jeans and made my way to the hotel. When I arrived, I saw an imposing escalator leading upward. As I ascended, I felt that I was being lifted out of my grieving state toward something greater. At the top, I met the executive who was not in a suit as I had imagined but was wearing a jersey, a platinum chain, matching earrings, and white Converse shoes. He stepped forward, extended his hand, smiled, and said, "What's up, man. My Name is Tru."

"Hi, I'm Bobby. Nice to meet you," I said. With that handshake, a 20-year friendship began, one that would shape my career, my family, and my life in ways I could never have imagined.

THE HARD GRIND AND SEEKING WISDOM FROM A MENTOR

Ten years had passed since our first meeting. Our small agency, led by Tru, had grown to become an industry leader and had been acquired. It was a new beginning for all of us. We were at our new company barely a year, and the holidays were approaching.

My phone rang. I saw it was Tru. I picked up the phone, expecting to talk about the next big project we needed to focus on closing for our next calendar year. Instead, when I asked Tru, "What's up?" he simply said, "Bro, I want to let you know I'm out."

I replied, "Wait, what do you mean you're out?"

He said, "I'm done. It was a mutual decision, and I'm out as the head of our group." I was stunned. Tru was the only person I had ever worked for in the agency world. He mentored me, taught me, and now he was telling me that he's leaving. I asked, "Well, who's taking over? What do you want to do?"

He replied, "I'm not sure who's going to take over, but I told them I think it should be you."

I was both humbled and terrified. What does that even mean? Me, run this multimillion-dollar agency? What was I going to be responsible for? I was honored that he thought I could do it and that he believed in my capabilities. But to be honest, I didn't even know if I wanted the job. The job of running an agency, or even a division within an agency, is demanding. Long hours, and you are responsible for the people, the profits, and the overall performance of the agency. The job never ends. It's like a Whac-A-Mole game: as soon as you feel you've solved one problem, another pops up immediately.

We continued our conversation, and I asked him, "What do you want to do?" He replied, "Not sure yet." He said he wanted to take some time to think about what he wanted to do with this next chapter. He said, "But I know this is the right time to move on. I think you'd be great at this role."

He assured me, "I'll always be here to support you in any way that you need. My guess is that they'll probably call you shortly to talk with the president."

I said, "Okay."

I told him that to be honest, I wasn't sure whether I wanted to do the job. He said, "I hear you. That's fine. But don't make up your mind yet. Give it some time. Think about it. Make a decision that you think is best for you." We hung up.

Within 30 minutes, the phone rang again, this time from a different corporate office. They asked me to meet them at the office later that day or first thing in the morning. I decided to give myself a good night's sleep and agreed to meet them in the office the next morning.

I thought about it, weighing the pros and cons of taking on the role. Ultimately, I decided that I was up for the challenge of running an agency. It seemed like the next level of growth for me, both professionally and personally. I was ready to embrace it. I went to the office the next day and met with the president of the agency and the leadership team. We discussed the role, and I shared my enthusiasm for taking it on. I saw it as an opportunity to create a new vision for the group.

They were happy to hear that I was up for the challenge and prepared to support me as needed. They proved to be a great resource.

After a short break for the holidays, I came back at the beginning of the year, ready to tackle my new role and face my new reality. Over the course of the year, we developed a new vision and strategy, and as a team, we got to work. We identified the right market opportunities, leading to rapid growth with new hires and new business opportunities.

We won so much business in our first year that we literally had to turn down new clients that wanted to work with us. We celebrated as a team, toasting to our success and growth. The organization was thrilled, but I was exhausted. The agency grind is never ending, and we didn't have time to dwell on our achievements.

The only real prize we got was the opportunity to do it all over again next year.

While writing *Good Is the New Cool* my perspective on what was possible for my career had changed—my aperture had widened. I thought about what we had to do to achieve that level of success year in and year out. Our performance demanded more travel and more work, and I realized that I was starting to hit a wall. The work we were doing was cool and fun, but it lacked meaning. I was really hungry for meaning.

I decided that I needed to find a Purpose in my life. I reached out to Tru for help.

I told him, "I don't know what I want to do. I can't do this anymore."

He replied, "Sounds like you're ready to go on a journey." I said, "I don't know where to start. I need a map."

He said, "You don't need a map. You need a compass. So, I think you'd be the perfect person to go through it."

It turned out that Tru had been working on a coaching practice to help people find their Purpose. It was the first time he had ever taken anyone on this particular journey, and he called it *GPS to Purpose*. Together, we went on a journey.

He said, "We'll meet every Saturday morning at 7 a.m. We will go on this journey together, and each week we'll talk, and you'll have assignments to complete before the next step in the journey."

He added, "We'll start this Saturday. Are you ready?" I thanked him and said, "I'm ready."

There was a certain excitement that I felt, a weight lifted from me simply by asking for help. And being vulnerable just made me feel so much less alone.

As I started to embark on my journey, I said a prayer: "God, I ask you for two things: give me the clarity to know what you want me to do, and give me the courage to do it." With that, my journey began.

BOBBY FINDS HIS GPS

Three weeks passed, and every Saturday I began to look forward to it. It actually made the weekdays easier because I knew I was working toward something hopeful, and I was excited about it.

Tru and I discussed my Gifts and how they could be shared with those around me—my superpowers, the things that other people truly appreciated about me. I asked family, friends, and colleagues, and I realized I have these Gifts:

- **The ability to inspire:** To motivate and uplift others through words, actions, and example.
- **Trustworthiness:** The reliability and integrity that others can depend on, knowing that I will uphold my commitments and be true to my word.

- **Calmness:** Creating perspective and mindfulness for myself and others, paying attention to the present moment without judgment.
- **Moral imagination:** Envisioning a full range of possibilities to solve ethical challenges in our lives and the world.
- **Creating connectedness:** Helping people to feel seen, heard, and connected to the good in themselves and others.
- **Storytelling:** Crafting expansive narratives for who we are and what we are capable of.
- **Perseverance:** Demonstrating an unstoppable will to keep going forward.

We then explored my Passions. What brought me alive and energized me? What broke my heart? I discovered I had a range of Passions:

- **Faith, fatherhood, and family:** These mattered most to me
- **Entrepreneurship:** Building brands and offerings that fill voids in the marketplace.
- **Education:** Both the pursuit of learning and the act of teaching.
- **Mentorship:** Making a positive impact in the lives of young people and helping others to fulfill their dreams.

It was exciting to see these words on a page. Even as I look back on them nine years later, they still feel true as a source of energy and enthusiasm. It's amazing to see how much of my life today is aligned with them.

We then moved to how I could specifically use my Gifts and Passions to be of Service. I thought about how I could be of Service to young people, peers, and others who wanted to live the best lives but didn't know how.

After six months, the final step in the journey was for me to write a Purpose statement, and I was excited to do this. This was why I had embarked on this journey—to uncover the road map to making the world a better place. But when I sat down to write it, I found it challenging. I was so eager to find a way to be of Service that I thought any statement would suffice. My first draft was "to make the world a better place." I figured, this is why I started on the journey in the first place, so why not?

When I shared it with Tru, he paused and told me it was okay but that it had to be unique to me and my journey. So I took a break and went back to work, unsure of what was missing. I thought some more over the next week and came back with another draft. I shared it with Tru, and again he paused and said it was better but still didn't feel that it was coming from deep within me. I started to feel dejected.

I had spent all these months trying to get clarity, and now I was stuck. I decided I needed to take a break. My mother was having knee surgery, and I was going back to Washington, DC, to take care of her. On my way back home to care for my mother, I started journaling in my notebook while on the train. Memories started to flood in, including one from a man named Eric Dawson.

My wife Renee had introduced us, and he was someone who had found his Purpose at a young age. He started a nonprofit called Peace Games, which later became Peace First. It was dedicated to empowering young people as peacemakers. I was drawn to their mission and started informally helping and advising them. When I met Eric, he exuded a certain presence that instantly connected with everyone he met. He was deeply committed to his work and grounded in it. I remembered a story he shared that triggered something within me.

The story goes:

An old Cherokee chief was teaching his grandson about life. "A fight is going on inside us," he said to the boy. "It is a terrible fight and is between two wolves."

"One is evil," he continued. "He is anger, envy, sorrow, regret, greed, arrogance, self-pity, guilt, resentment, inferiority, lies, false pride, superiority, and ego."

He paused, and then said, "The other is good. He is joy, peace, love, hope, serenity, humility, kindness, benevolence, empathy, generosity, truth, compassion, and faith."

The grandson thought about this for a minute and then asked his grandfather, "Which wolf will win?"

The old Cherokee simply replied, "The one you feed."

As I was traveling, thoughts of everything I wanted my work to achieve and how I wanted it to be done filled my mind. It became clear that I wanted my work to combat divisiveness, hatred, anger, selfishness, and greed. I wanted it to contribute to my Passion, love, and bringing out the best in people. Without even realizing it, I filled pages and pages in my notebook. And at the end of it all, my hand stopped, and I looked down at the page. The last line simply said, *"I exist to serve by feeding the good wolf in myself and others."*

It was simple, clear, and aligned with everything that flowed from my heart and soul. It represented who I wanted to be, how I wanted to live, and the impact I wanted to make. I couldn't believe it was true. I read it to Tru, expecting to hear, once again a pregnant pause. But instead, he seemed to light up and said, "Bro, this is you. This is your work. This is your Purpose. I've known you for ten years, and I can't think of a more perfect statement."

I became emotional and thanked him, even though those words felt inadequate to express my gratitude. I felt a sense of hope and possibility, a clarity that I had been searching for.

BOBBY SHARES HIS STORY WITH AFDHEL

By this stage in my life, a profound transformation had taken place. Clarity of Purpose had enriched my existence, and each day was a testament to this newfound mission. Though work presented its fair share of challenges, every hurdle felt like a step toward something that truly mattered.

One day, as I sat down for a conversation with Afdhel, I could sense his gaze analyzing the change in me. "You seem lighter and happier," he remarked with a curious twinkle in his eyes. The warmth of his observation made me proud, and I enthusiastically shared my journey.

I began sharing the odyssey of self-discovery I had embarked on—my *GPS to Purpose* journey with Tru. With an air of awe, I shared the intricate process, the nuggets of wisdom I gathered along the way, and how it all converged to give me the clarity that had been eluding me for so long.

As I recounted my story, I noticed Afdhel leaning in closer, his expression a mix of fascination and yearning. It became evident that Afdhel, too, stood at the crossroads where I had once found myself. He was gripped by the same thirst for meaning that had propelled me on my quest.

With a voice tinged with hope, Afdhel inquired if he could meet Tru, as he wished to explore his own path to Purpose.

I offered him an encouraging smile, feeling an indescribable sense of fulfillment. It was as if my journey had come full circle; not only had it brought about my own enlightenment but it was now also serving as a beacon for others in search of their Purpose.

AF GOES ON HIS OWN JOURNEY TO FIND PURPOSE

When I found out about Bobby's incredible journey with Tru, I knew I had to go on it myself. I knew I was reaching the end of my tether with corporate life. While I had successfully managed to incorporate positive and meaningful elements into my work—for instance, partnering the brands I managed with nonprofits to raise money—I felt that I could stretch my wingspan further.

So I embarked on the same process with Tru, the deep self-exploration and understanding of what was important to me at this stage in my life and my career.

I loved the work with Tru. He was a combination of priest and coach, always gently encouraging, using wisdom and humor to push me out of my comfort zone.

After many weeks of coaching with Tru, looking at my own Gifts, Passions, and Service, I had uncovered the following:

- **My Gifts:** Storytelling in all its forms. I had loved the creativity of telling stories from a young age. I've written books of poetry and fiction, short stories, and newspaper articles. I've created content and experiences for brands that told their story in compelling and exciting ways.
- **My Passion:** Ever since writing the first book, I had discovered a newfound Passion for the idea of brands and business being a force for good, and I was excited by the idea of spreading the word.
- **My Service:** I realized I could be of Service to the hundreds of thousands of marketers and business leaders like me, who were also struggling with finding meaning in what they did for a living.

After weeks of thinking, I wrote down a Purpose statement, which at first glance looked illogical and circular.

"My Purpose is to inspire Purpose in people and organizations."

Reading it out made me confused: how could my Purpose revolve around spreading the message about Purpose to others?

But the more I read it and sat with it, the more it made sense to me—and thrilled me with the magnitude of the task, one that I could never fully accomplish in my lifetime.

Looking back at this statement from the vantage point of 2024 gives me goosebumps.

It led to me understanding all the many ways I could bring that Purpose to life: from speaking around the world (using storytelling on stage) to writing for *Forbes* (telling stories of inspiring brands and businesses) to consulting (helping inspire brands and businesses see and live a new story about themselves—one that helped them grow by solving the world's problems).

Having this level of personal clarity gave me a sense of courage—and a blueprint to execute, which I was lucky enough to mostly achieve.

It gave me the courage to quit my corporate job on January 1, 2017.

I had six months of savings, and a wife and three-year-old son who were depending on me to provide for them. It was a pretty terrifying prospect, and I wasn't quite sure what I was going to do next.

But the success of what happened next was due to some amazing allies who the universe sent our way to help us.

One of them came via an email out of the blue—from Slovenia of all places.

CHAPTER 3

LIVING
OUR PURPOSE

> And, when you want something with all of your heart, all the
> universe conspires in helping you to achieve it.
> —Paulo Coelho, The Alchemist

That email came from a woman called Nadia Laurinci—a petite, plucky powerhouse with a sparkling grin.

The email said: "I saw your TEDx Bushwick Talk and I think you could be a professional speaker. Can we set up a meeting?"

The talk she was referring to was my first noncorporate talk I had done around the theme of *Good Is the New Cool*. It was my attempt to turn the book into a keynote talk and it was *terrible*.

I was sweating under the hot lights of the tiny stage in Bushwick, Brooklyn.

I was stuttering and stammering and definitely not polished.

(In fact, the video was so bad that years later I begged the TEDx organization to take it down; such was my embarrassment at it.)

TURNING PURPOSE INTO PROSPERITY

By some miracle of the universe, Nadia had seen it all the way in Europe, and something in that video, however raw and unpolished it was, had struck a chord.

A few weeks later, Bobby and I were meeting Nadia at Soho House New York. She ran a professional speaking agency, managing many amazing scientists, business leaders, and innovators, and she wanted to add us to the roster.

To be honest, the thought of getting paid as a professional speaker had never really crossed my mind. I enjoyed speaking in public and felt no fear at standing up in front of an audience of strangers.

But the first time I spoke professionally—at the IEG Sponsorship Conference in Chicago in April 2017—and have someone present me with a check for a month's salary for the 45 minutes I had just done on stage, a light bulb went off in my head.

I could do this. I could make a living speaking passionately about my ideas on how business can be a force for good—and I could get paid enough money to support my family.

Nadia was the game changer who enabled me to do that. She managed every aspect of my speaking business—negotiating deals, handling contracts, having her team book my travel—so that I could just concentrate on fine-tuning my message and lighting up audiences.

I started traveling the world speaking at conferences and companies from Tel Aviv to Peru, from Vancouver to Stockholm. I keynoted 30–40 times a year, spending nights sleeping on economy class seats, fueling my body with coffee so I could make it on stage the next day and deliver my message.

I sometimes joked that my clients weren't paying me to speak; they were paying me to travel. (And yes, don't worry, I eventually found ways to carbon offset all those airmiles I was racking up!)

This time though, when I spoke to my son Nuri and explained what I was doing, I could hold my head up high. I could tell him that I was flying to these places to help inspire people to do more good in the world, to take the enormous power of these corporations that they were part of and use them in service of making the world a better place.

BOBBY TAKES A LEAP OF FAITH

My work with Tru had blessed me with clarity. Now I needed to find where and how to actually live this out. I went back to my agency work, but it felt different. I was like Neo in *The Matrix* going back to work after taking the red pill. Nothing looked the same anymore. Every task, every meeting, every RFP just felt further away from the work I was now clearly called to do.

I started to think about when my work felt most meaningful. Young people and their well-being had always been a Passion of mine. Moments that stood out were when I was in meetings at Peace First as an advisor, helping them to think of new possibilities to unleash the moral imaginations of young people. So I called Eric Dawson, and he responded saying he would be in New York and wanted to catch up to see how I was doing. It was December when we met at my building.

He simply asked, "How are you doing?" But I paused and told him about my recent journey and the clarity I had found in my Purpose. In that moment, I felt called to feed the good and make a positive impact. Eric seemed amazed by my journey and the clarity I had attained. He spoke about a light he saw in me and said, "You feel grounded. You seem hopeful."

I asked him how he was doing, and he revealed that he was at his own crossroads. At 41 years old, he had been leading Peace First since he was a teen and felt that he had taken it as far as he could. The current model focused on teaching young people how to be peacemakers through educational curricula, but it didn't seem big enough to meet the challenges and opportunities of this moment. Billions of young people were hungry to make positive change but lacked the resources, community, and support to bring their ideas to reality. Peace First needed to grow to meet the power of this moment.

We both agreed that we wanted to do something bigger. Eric said that I had always had a bolder vision for Peace First, expanding its impact and reach. He was ready to create something in line with that magnitude. He recognized that I had a calling for this work. So he proposed that we build this next chapter of Peace First together. I expressed uncertainty about what it would look like, but we agreed to figure it out together. We decided to take some time during the holidays to think it through and reconvene in January.

He said, "I don't know what this can look like, but I think we can figure this out together." We both said we would take a break to think about it over the holidays. We came back together in January. We decided to spend the next several months fleshing out what our partnership could look like.

As I went back to work, it became clear to me that it was time for me to move on from my job. The company had been good to me, but I had a different calling. For months, I continued to do my work, delivering great results for our clients and continuing to grow the business.

But I had also begun to imagine what the rest of my life's work would look like. Over six months, Eric and I fleshed out what my role could be and what it could look like. At the end, he said he was going to send me a job description. He wanted me to look at it, and if all looked good, they would make me an offer.

I checked my inbox that week, and there was an email from Eric. The subject line read "Peace First CMO." I read through the traditional list of qualification requirements. Then it read, "Job Description." The first line simply said, *"As Chief Marketing Officer, your job is to feed the good in young people throughout the world."*

I couldn't believe it! The job description for the role was *literally* my Purpose statement. I was going to work to fulfill my Purpose every day. Honestly, I don't even remember reading the rest of the job description. I'm sure I did at some point, but at that moment I knew with absolute clarity that this was the work I needed to do. I had asked for clarity and got it. Now the next step was to have the courage to actually do it.

This was going to require me to take the biggest leap of faith I had ever taken. I was going to leave a world that I had known my whole professional life and step into a new world of the unknown, doing something that in many ways I had never done, for an organization that I had never worked for, at a scale that I had never imagined. I had to have the courage to not only make the decision to walk away but to communicate that decision to people I had been working with, including the team—people who had become almost like family.

I was worried about what the reaction was going to be and the typical disappointment and sometimes anger that comes when people leave. But I made the call. Although everyone was disappointed I was leaving, when I told them what I was going to do, they all, in their own way, told me that I had to go and do that work. They supported me. They encouraged me. They took me out to a celebratory lunch. I packed up my things, my boxes, and headed out the door.

I left my old world holding a box of my belongings in my hands and a new world, a new chapter, held in my heart and mind. The next day I started as the CMO at Peace First.

SPREADING THE WORD

Afdhel and Bobby Speak at SXSW.

After the book came out, we began to experience an exciting whirlwind of invitations to speak and to share more about our book with different communities and audiences. It was an exciting time being able to share our story with people who were genuinely interested in our journeys—but also in this new model we were offering ideas that they could apply to their lives and their work in ways that could bring them a greater sense of fulfillment and meaning.

We also began to create submissions for places where we thought our message could resonate. We didn't know whether those submissions would ever be accepted, but we figured it was worth a shot. One of these was South by Southwest. We had been to South by Southwest several years earlier as marketers doing events and activations, but we had never been there as speakers. So we thought that this was an opportunity to create a different experience for ourselves, and we submitted an application to do a talk at South by Southwest. A few weeks later, we were excited to find out that we had been accepted. It was a simple email that we received, inviting us to register.

We received the message, an email that simply said, "2017 SXSW Speaker Agreement." We couldn't believe it! We had been selected as speakers for South by Southwest to share our book, *Good Is the New Cool*. We were beyond excited, and as we began to get ready for our trip, it was another reminder of how amazing this journey was turning out to be. But yet again, similar doubts and fears emerged. *I mean, it's great that South by Southwest wants us, but what if no one comes? How embarrassing would it be to have to speak to an empty room? What if no one really cares about this book or this session?* We would have wasted our time coming all the way to South by Southwest, traveling all the way to Austin. *Surely that can't be the case—surely, we didn't come all this way just to embarrass ourselves? Were we about to look like losers?*

As we started packing our bags and preparing for the trip, doubts continued to cloud our minds. When we walked into the convention center, we saw a poster with our faces on it, which said, "Good Is the New Cool" Session starting at 3 p.m. We took pictures of ourselves in the convention center, feeling excited and like we were about to embark on this new journey. We met our host, who took us to the green room, where we sat with other speakers who were also nervously anticipating their upcoming sessions.

About 10 minutes before we went on stage, Bobby went outside to go to the bathroom. As he walked through the hall, there was this long line of people waiting to get into one of the, presumably other, sessions. As he walked from the end of the line to the front of it on his way to the restroom, he began thinking to himself, "Look at all these people going for this other talk. This is the reason why our session is going to be empty because everybody's going to this one." It felt like a bad omen. As he kept walking, he grew more disheartened. The only line that he saw with people was for this other speaker's session and not ours. As he walked to the front, he became increasingly curious about who everyone was so excited to see.

He asked someone, "What session is this?" The person looked at him and smiled and said, "This is for the *Good Is the New Cool* session."

He couldn't believe it! His eyes got wide; his jaw dropped. He looked at the line again and said, "This line is for us!" (He was so excited that he forgot he had to use the bathroom.)

We could not believe that this was the turnout for our session—a line going all the way down the convention hall and wrapped around the corner, all to learn more about our book. We stood at the doorway when the session opened, gratefully greeting each person for choosing to spend their precious conference time with us, and as the room filled, so did our hearts.

As we began to see the impact that this book was starting to have, for 45 minutes we stood on stage, shared stories, laughed, and imagined. We took questions, and after the event there was a book signing. There was another line of people, again wrapped in a long line, some with books they had already purchased in hand, some buying books at the stand, but each of them was standing in line for a moment to meet us and to share a message about why the book mattered to them.

It was one of the most incredible feelings we'd had on this journey. And as the last person left, we said thank you, and we looked at each other and just said, "Well done, brother."

CRASHING BACK TO REALITY

The rest of the story after South by Southwest though is worth mentioning to share the hard new realities that we were facing. After the incredible experience, the reality set in for me: I had to fly from Austin, Texas, to Toronto, Canada, for a speaking engagement in two days.

I flew from Austin to Orlando to catch a connecting flight. But a massive winter storm had shut down the airport, and when I arrived there, it was chaos.

Every single hotel room had been booked solid by the tens of thousands of travelers who were stranded. And this time I had no corporate travel desk to help me find a place to stay. I was on my own. I trudged around the airport hotels in the area, trying to find a room for the night with zero luck.

I was back in the airport terminal, sitting on a bench, looking at the information board, which just said:

FLIGHT CANCELED
FLIGHT CANCELED
FLIGHT CANCELED

For the foreseeable future.

There was absolutely nothing I could do. No one I could turn to for help.

I looked down at the bench I was slumped on and realized that it was going to be my bed for the night. So I laid down my suitcase as my pillow, covered myself in my coat, and tried to get some sleep.

By some miracle the next day when the flights reopened, I was able to get a connecting flight to Toronto that got me there just in time, and I delivered my keynote.

But I never forgot that crucible moment for me. It was a moment that signaled my determination to keep going in this chosen life, no matter what the setbacks and obstacles were.

To this day, every time I fly through Orlando, I make it a point to walk past that same bench. My fingers touch it lightly, as if it were a talisman.

It reminds me to stay strong, to stay true to my Purpose.

TURNING INSPIRATION INTO ACTION
How We Started Conspiracy of Love to Help Brands and Companies

In the meantime, something else was happening because of the speaking. We were invited to share our message with some of the world's largest companies. Companies such as Mars, Mondelez, and PepsiCo were seeing the same data we were seeing about this tectonic shift in consumer values, wanting brands to become more conscious and empathetic.

After we had finished speaking, we started to get requests from the leaders at these companies: hey, you guys know so much about this topic; why don't you come and help us?

And it is from these humble beginnings that our consultancy, Conspiracy of Love, was born. Believe it or not, the name was originally a URL that Afdhel had bought for an electronic music project. But it turned out to be an accidentally perfect metaphor for what we stood for.

We realized that companies were very good at asking for love: they wanted to be the best-loved brand, they wanted their employees to say that they loved working there.

But what these companies didn't seem to quite understand was that they had to give love in order to get love.

They had to show love to their employees by creating safe places to do meaningful work, where people felt that they belonged and had value.

Their brands had to show love for their customers, showing how they stood up for their values and "solve problems from the everyday to the epic," as our book had preached.

The companies themselves had to show love for their communities and the planet, genuinely helping make the world a better place, both environmentally and socially.

So we embarked on a new role: consulting with these brands as they went on a journey to find their own Purpose and bring it to life in authentic ways.

Inspired brand marketers, with hearts swelling with the desire to contribute, began seeking advice on how to make a positive impact during these trying times. We helped Oreo embark on a mission to alleviate the loneliness that permeated the air, Ritz collaborated with Feeding America to ensure no family went hungry, Triscuit strove to bring nutritious ingredients to food deserts, Sour Patch Kids bestowed scholarships to visionary changemakers at Historically Black Colleges and Universities, Crown Royal extended their unwavering support to veterans, and the list goes on.

Over time, Conspiracy of Love has helped major corporations invest millions of dollars into causes such as racial justice in education, food insecurity, childhood hunger, and arts education, partnering them with leading nonprofits such as Feeding America, the Boys and Girls Clubs of America, the Thurgood Marshall College Fund, and many others.

It's a legacy that we look back on and marvel.

Our vision did come true. "Good" did become the new "cool."

And we were at the right time in the right place, helping inspire some of the biggest brands and companies on the planet to do more good in tangible and measurable ways.

NURTURING A COMMUNITY OF CHANGEMAKERS

Creating the first Good Is the New Cool Conference at TOMS Shoes HQ

The book and consultancy had opened up myriad avenues for us to help people, and we felt a responsibility to keep the momentum going.

We decided to establish a community for like-minded individuals who were passionate about creating positive change through their work. Our aim was to foster a community where leaders from the world of brands, nonprofits, and culture could share their ideas and experiences, and support each other.

As the community grew, we found ourselves in a position to influence and mentor the next generation of changemakers. We conducted workshops and webinars and initiated collaborations with educational institutions.

But we felt that there was room for something even bigger. There was a hunger among the community to get to know each other, not feel as if they were the only people out there trying to change their businesses and their world for the better.

We missed that electricity in the room when something magical was happening.

We drew on our experience creating cultural events for brands and decided to try and create our own Good Is the New Cool event, where we could bring the lessons of the book to life.

Our very first GoodCon event took place at the TOMS Shoes Headquarters in Los Angeles. We couldn't think of a more fitting place than a company that we deeply admired as a shining example of a new model of business as a force for good.

We invited thought leaders that we admired to come and share their journey and wisdom:

Robert Egger, a pioneer who had started DC Kitchen and LA Kitchen to feed thousands, came and lit the room on fire with his bold and blunt rhetoric.

Eunique Jones Gibson shared her journey to building Because of Them We Can into a platform that helps African Americans see and be their best selves.

Zenia Tata, the chief impact officer of X Prize, talked to David Hertz, winner of the Water Abundance X Prize for his invention, a device that could extract at least 2,000 liters of water a day from the atmosphere.

We ended the day with a soul-stirring performance by Marisa Hamamoto and her disabled dance troupe, which ended with all of the audience joining the performers on the dance floor in one joyous celebration.

We remember being on cloud nine that day. We had given our community what it needed: a moment of togetherness, joy, inspiration.

Attendees felt changed for the better and ready to make a difference with new tools and friends. One person said, "At GoodCon, I found my people, and I found myself."

But little did we know that this was just the beginning.

Sitting in the audience were two women—Shani Langi and Sharice Bellantonio—who had flown all the way from Australia to be with us. They ran a hugely successful events business. After the event they came to us and invited us to come and do GoodCon events in Sydney and Melbourne later that year, which were powerful experiences showing us the worldwide hunger there was for this mix of inspiration, innovation, and impact.

That led to us doing GoodCon events around the world. We did them in London at the Conduit Club, a gathering spot for UK-based changemakers. We did them in New York, in collaboration with the United Nations. And we came back to Los Angeles a few years later, kicking off with a very special guest appearance by none other than Malala Yousafzai, one of our heroes.

Also sitting in the audience that day at TOMS was another wonderful human being who would change our lives for the better—the phenomenal Helen Trickey, who went on to become one of our managing partners of Conspiracy of Love.

And a few years later, Los Angeles was the place where we met Philipp Reker, a whip-smart and passionate German who worked at Mattel and who also joined us at Conspiracy as the other managing partner.

It's amazing how the universe brings you the right people into your life just when you need them.

Looking back, the inception of *Good Is the New Cool* was more than just the creation of a book; it was the beginning of a movement. It was a testament that with Passion, persistence, and a bit of luck, everyday people collaborating together can make a positive impact in the world.

Together with the creation of Conspiracy of Love, it was what allowed us to turn our Purpose into prosperity: to help us and our teams create lives of meaning and freedom, where we could create our best lives and our best work in balance and harmony.

The journey continues, as we constantly seek new stories, insights, and opportunities to create meaningful change. We remain grounded and committed to the belief that "good" can indeed be the new cool and that through creativity and collaboration, we can all contribute to a better world.

However, in early 2020, as winter clung to the northern hemisphere, a shadow began to creep across the globe. What had started as a distant whisper from the city of Wuhan in China swiftly turned into a tsunami of fear and uncertainty. The name COVID-19, an unfamiliar and scientific term, began to permeate news outlets and conversations as steadily as the virus itself infiltrated communities.

CHAPTER 4

THE WORLD SHUTS DOWN

Disaster strikes: The COVID-19 pandemic. Our grand plans seemed to dissipate before our very eyes.

Gone was the gentle buzz of daily life. As governments began to grasp the severity of the pandemic, they pulled on the emergency brakes. Streets that once teemed with the frenzy of daily commutes, cheerful coffee shop chatter, and children's laughter turned hauntingly silent. The vibrant mosaic of city lights dimmed, as the doors of businesses and institutions slammed shut. The world, with its unending rhythm, seemed to have stumbled and paused.

Skies, once crisscrossed with the contrails of countless airplanes, cleared up as international travel shrunk to a mere trickle. What used to be an age of unparalleled interconnectedness suddenly felt like a bygone era. Airports, which had epitomized the globalized world, stood like ghost towns, their usually bustling halls echoing emptiness.

Social distancing, a term which had been alien to most, became the rule of human interaction. Face masks, previously associated with hospitals and pollution, became as necessary as shoes and phones when leaving home. Hand sanitizers and toilet paper morphed into precious commodities, as panicked shoppers stripped grocery store shelves bare.

Within households, the palpable tension grew. Families, now confined within their homes, scrambled to create a semblance of normalcy. The aroma of home-cooked meals wafted through homes more frequently, but so did the despair of isolation. The sounds of keyboards and video calls replaced the human connection that workplaces offered. Children, unable to grasp the enormity of what was happening, attended school through screens, their joyful recesses replaced by digital backdrops.

Meanwhile, hospitals became battlefields. The harrowed faces of health care workers, etched with exhaustion and despair, became emblematic of the crisis. Clad in layers of protective gear, they fought tirelessly to save lives even as the relentless wave of infections threatened to drown them. The nightly applause and clanging pots from balconies were a testament to their valor.

In the quietude, nature seemed to breathe a sigh of relief. With the world momentarily at a standstill, pollution levels plummeted, and wildlife ventured into territories they had long forsaken. Crystal clear waters and azure skies reappeared, a poignant reminder of the Earth's inherent resilience.

As weeks turned into months, the global populace found itself navigating a new and uncertain landscape. The streets may have been silent, but behind closed doors, humanity grappled with grief, discovery, adaptation, and resilience. The world, collectively holding its breath, began to realize that what lay ahead was a transformative journey.

A MAN NAMED GEORGE FLOYD

Bobby Marches with His Son—and Faces His Own Moment on the Streets

When I think back to writing our second book, *The Good Is the New Cool Guide to Conscious Business*, I think a lot about what was happening outside my window in 2020. It was one of the most eventful periods in world history. And so many of those events were brought to life right outside my window, living in Brooklyn, New York.

At the time, New York was part of the epicenter of the COVID-19 pandemic. People were getting sick and dying at historic levels. There was tremendous pain and suffering in New York and around the world. Like many others, I was quarantined inside my home with my family. And during this period of not knowing how long this was going to last, I was trying to find a way to be useful, just trying to figure out how I could do something that helps someone.

I remember sitting in my bedroom often, thinking about the book, and as I wrote it every day, the walls felt as if they were closing in on me.

But outside that room, something started to happen.

Around six o'clock every day there would be this moment where people in my building would open their windows and begin to cheer. All of this was happening as a sign of gratitude and appreciation for the frontline workers. And I remember the first couple of days being deeply moved by it, and then I began to do it with my family.

We would open the doors and go outside, and we would clap and yell. Those daily moments when people celebrated our heroes gave me such a sense of inspiration and connection to many others.

And I wanted to write something that captured that moment and connected to those who wanted to do something to leave our world better than they found it.

One day, I was sitting at home and was on my computer, and a story popped up. The story was not about COVID-19. It was about this image of a man named George Floyd, who was killed that day by a police officer. And I remember just being intensely haunted by it, the callousness of it, the coldness of it.

I was looking at this officer kneeling on the neck of this Black man pleading for his life.

And I was angry and utterly outraged, but I didn't know what to do with that anger and frustration. I sat down that day to write, not necessarily knowing what to say, what to write, feeling very distracted by what I was feeling.

And so, I was looking forward to that six o'clock break where people would open their windows, cheer, and bang on pots and pans. Six o'clock came, but there was a different sound. I heard people yelling and cheering, but I also listened to this phrase repeatedly.

It started as a whisper, and then it just kept getting louder and louder: "No justice, no peace, no justice, no peace."

And you could hear the chorus. You could hear the voices of the people. You could hear the footsteps, which kept getting louder and louder. It was like a wave of people flooding the streets, holding signs, and raising their voices. The rhythm, the power, the anger, the raw emotion—it all felt like a surge washing over me, amplified by the sheer number of participants. This was unlike any march or protest I had ever experienced. I remember standing there, realizing that I was witnessing a wave of change, and I felt profoundly connected to it.

They marched daily. One day, I sat down by the window with my son Miles, who was nine years old at the time, and talked about it. I said, "We're going to go down together, and we are going to march." At first, he didn't want to; he was afraid, understandably.

And I said, "Well, it's important that we do this, so we're going to do it together. We don't have to march the whole time. Whenever you're ready to come back home, we'll come back home." He said okay, and we went downstairs. I could feel him tensing up because there were thousands of people marching.

But just like any wave, you find your place in it.

We got in the streets, and we marched. We walked together, holding hands. We joined that chorus of "no justice, no peace." We said it together. As we walked, I flashed back to so many experiences I had in my own life, where I've felt uneasy with the police.

I thought about this particular experience when Miles and I were together the year before on the streets of Brooklyn.

He was eight at the time and having an emotional meltdown on the street as we walked home from playing at the YMCA, as children sometimes do. My wife was away on a trip, and Miles was hungry, tired, and missing his mom. Evidently, he was yelling too much for someone watching us on the street, who decided it would be a good idea to call the police to quiet him down.

Suddenly sirens and flashing lights surrounded us as police cars drove up. I was focused on trying to calm Miles down and didn't pay much attention to them as it was a busy street that we were on with police cars all the time. When the police cars turned around, I realized those police officers were there for us. I saw two police officers walking toward me straight ahead, another pair of officers walking to my left, and another officer walking from my right. The officer on the right had a taser. I thought to myself in disbelief, "There's no way that all of these officers are here to handle a child having a tantrum right now."

As the officers approached, I remembered everything my parents had taught me about dealing with the police: staying calm, using an even tone of voice, saying, "Yes, officer," "No, officer"—while being so angry that this was even happening. One of the officers asked, "What's happening?" and I just explained that my son was upset. He's a child having a moment. I told them, "It seems excessive to have all this police presence for this."

There was another officer, a woman. She directed a question to my son and asked, "Are you okay?" And he said, "I'm okay." Then she said, "What's wrong?" And he talked about his day. He spoke about the fact that his teacher told him that he couldn't play when he wanted to play and couldn't go outside when he wanted to go outside and that he missed his mom. And I don't know if she was a mother or someone who could connect with him, but she saw him as this child who just wanted his mother. She told all the other officers to leave. She said to Miles, "You know, you will be okay. I want you guys to go home and get home safe." And so we did.

And as we were marching on this day and in this crowd, and again, walking and chanting, I thought about that incident. And I thought about George Floyd and the fact that as this officer was kneeling on his neck, George was pleading for his life, and while he was dying, he was calling for his mother, who was all *he* wanted at that moment.

I realized how important what we were doing was.

And I pulled Miles out of the crowd and said, "I want you to understand why we're marching. There is a thing in this world called justice.

There's equality; there are things that are right and things that are wrong. And when things are unjust and not right, you have a responsibility to help change that. And so we're marching for you. We're marching for all your friends; we're marching for all of our family. And you see all these people are marching together? We're marching for their friends and family. And it's important that you understand the responsibility that when you see people who are fighting for you, also fight to stand up for them. That is the power that you have. There is power in the people, there is power in our voice, and there is power in our actions. And I want you always to understand the power that you have. I never want you to feel powerless. I never want you to feel hopeless."

And I asked him, "Do you understand?" He looked at me and said, "I do." I said, "Change will only happen if you help make it happen. I want you to promise me you will." And he did.

We went home, and I wrote. I realized that Purpose and change aren't always pretty or glamorous. It's connected to much frustration and pain, but it is about channeling those emotions to create and envision something better.

My work is deeply connected to a sense of hope. And that's what I felt as I was writing. I hoped that what I was writing during this time would help. I thought about those people in the streets. Those people had jobs. They came from all walks of life. And as much as they're marching and protesting, they also want to do work that matters and that makes an impact in the world. And I thought about how I could help them do that.

I'm not a politician, so I'm not someone who's going to change policy directly. I don't know all the different levers of political power. But I do know business. I understand culture, and I see the power that business and culture have.

And so I can be of Service to those people who want to use the power of business and the power of culture to create change. I can help them do so.

It's in the act of Service that, even in those moments throughout that tumultuous year, I always found my sense of Purpose in this work. The work I've done and continue to do is all connected to that sense of hope, that unwavering belief in people's power to create change and my commitment to helping them do it.

I hope that this book does that. I hope it helps people when they go to work, or when they create companies, or when they start these new enterprises, or whatever audacious ideas they have.

I hope that it helps them to be the forces for good and forces for change that they want to be and it allows them to create the change they want to make.

FINDING SALVATION IN SERVICE

How We Tried to Help Our Community during the Pandemic

During the bleakness that enveloped 2020, we found salvation through Service and solidarity. Our consultancy, Conspiracy of Love, served as a catalyst for change and Passion. We launched a webinar series named *The Briefing*, which brought marketers from all walks of life together to brainstorm and learn about how they could employ the influence of their brands to combat the effects of the pandemic. Thousands of individuals participated, igniting a spark that would turn into a roaring flame of goodwill.

In tandem, we fostered our community through *Good Is the New Cool*, where people from over 40 countries connected in virtual events that we called GOODCon events. This community became a tapestry of hope, woven together by individuals determined to make a difference.

Our virtual talks reverberated across the globe, enabling individuals and organizations to unearth the treasure of Purpose lying dormant within them.

And we decided to use the time to write another book, using the time that we had forced on us to regroup and consider what was missing in the space of impact—an accessible and practical guide for corporate leaders wishing to transform their companies into Purpose-driven ones.

We penned what is now the *Good Is the New Cool Guide to Conscious Business: How Companies Can Drive Growth through Positive Impact.* It was designed to be a guiding light for corporate leaders to navigate the tumultuous seas of transforming their companies into forces for good growth. We wanted to create the first detailed road map for corporate leaders wishing to unleash the power of Purpose to achieve inspired innovation, engaged employees, and new frontiers for growth.

We interviewed inspiring leaders at companies such as Tesla, Patagonia, IKEA, Lego, Mattel, Chobani, and so many others where we could see inspiring examples of Purpose take place. To be clear—none of these companies is perfect, just like no human being is perfect.

But in each example, we were able to find the nugget of insight that we could turn into evergreen "principles of Purpose" for leaders to follow.

- Principles such as "Purpose must start inside out" encourage leaders to get their own house in order and take care of their employees first before trying to make the world better.
- Principles such as "Purpose is about picking your sword vs shields" help companies better prioritize between their *shields* (defensive issues) versus their *sword* (the biggest social or environmental problem in the world it could solve profitably).
- Principles such as "Be the helper, not the hero" encourage businesses to take a more humble posture, acting as enablers and facilitators to help turn their consumers into "heroes" changing the world.

Beyond strategies and theories, at the heart of all these initiatives was the embodiment of our intention to grow businesses through positive societal impact. The cultural zeitgeist during these uncertain times profoundly influenced us. Our mission transcended us. It was a clarion call for those who sought to be changemakers—not just in the streets but also in boardrooms and conference halls. We recognize that activism is not confined to marches; it thrives in the heart of business.

Our work emanates from the soul of activism. Our chosen canvas is the intersection of business and culture. We seek to empower those who yearn to wield the twin swords of business acumen and cultural influence to usher in change.

During the times when darkness seemed impenetrable, it was the act of helping and serving others that became our guiding light. Our belief in the innate power of individuals to bring about change, coupled with an unwavering commitment, remained our North Star.

The only thing that got us through was being of Service to others. We are proud that our book and our actions helped serve as the wind beneath the wings of countless dreamers and doers, as they forged ahead as champions of change, utilizing their talents and resources to build bridges, heal hearts, and transform the world for the better.

PEOPLE ARE HUNGRY FOR PURPOSE

Why We Wrote the Book You Are Holding

Globally, there's a palpable shift as individuals increasingly yearn for a sense of Purpose, particularly in the aftermath of the pandemic.

The pandemic acted as a magnifying glass on the facets of life that truly matter. First and foremost, it impelled a reevaluation of priorities.

No longer are people content with solely clocking in hours; they seek employers whose values echo their own, who support their well-being and sense of belonging, and whose mission contributes positively to society. The pandemic has unveiled the significance of our interconnectedness, community, and the impact of collective effort.

Moreover, the pandemic underscored the brevity of life, prompting many to aspire for more than just a paycheck. There's a growing refusal to settle for jobs that don't resonate with inner values and aspirations. Individuals are actively seeking roles that not only align with their belief system but also instill a sense of Purpose and meaning—not just a daily grind in Service of an abstract quarterly profit goal.

Additionally, the sense of community and solidarity fostered during the pandemic has accentuated the desire to be part of something larger. There's an escalating demand for companies with a backbone of social responsibility, driven to make the world a better place.

Envision a society where individual Gifts and Passions are not harnessed merely for personal gain but as invaluable tools for societal enrichment, where everyone is an artisan, intricately weaving their strengths into a tapestry of change and innovation. In this society, talents flourish, and Passions serve as the catalyst for transformative change. Engaging in Purpose-driven work becomes an act of responsibility, where individuals contribute to a harmonious and diverse symphony addressing the challenges of our time.

This alignment fosters innovation, cultivates empathy, and fortifies resilience. It not only nourishes the soul of the individual but sends ripples through humanity.

As pioneers who have personally experienced the transformational power of aligning Gifts and Passions to be of Service with a higher Purpose, we recognize this as a pivotal moment in time.

That's why we decided to write this book. To take the transformative idea that Tru created and to merge it with the work that we have done for seven years in some of the biggest and most iconic companies on the planet, helping their employees find Purpose and meaning.

And bring it to you so you could go on your own journey.

Ready to get started?

PART II

WHAT
IS PURPOSE?

In this section, we explain what individual Purpose is in the simplest possible terms.

It can feel like a giant, intimidating topic, but don't worry; over the years we've found a way to explain it in a fun and accessible way.

We introduce some key truths about Purpose that will help illuminate how to think about it so that when it's your turn to do your own GPS (in the last section), you are inspired and ready to get started.

CHAPTER 5

THE DEFINITION OF INDIVIDUAL PURPOSE

"This is the true joy in life, the being used for a Purpose
recognized by yourself as a mighty one."
–George Bernard Shaw

I t turns out first of all that Purpose is an ancient concept. It shows up
in myriad different cultures around the world.

For instance, in ancient Sanskrit it would be called your *Dharma*,
which translates as "courageous duty."

The ancient Greek philosopher Aristotle taught the philosophy of
eudaemonia, which spoke of the "pursuit of virtue, excellence, and the
best within us."

In Japanese, there is a wonderful concept called *"Ikigai"*: "Iki" in
Japanese means life and "gai" describes value or worth. So it translates
as your "life value" or "life worth."

In French, it is called your *"raison d'être,"* which translates to "your
reason for being."

It is your North Star, your guiding light, your compass that helps you
prioritize what to do with your time and energy on a daily basis.

Here's our definition of *personal Purpose:*

*Your reason for being in this moment, that gives you a sense of clarity,
courage, and focus and inspires how you can be of service to others and
the world.*

That phrase "in this moment" is an important part to unpack.

We've found it helpful to think of Purpose as a direction, not a destination. Your life's Purpose is more about the journey and the way you
live each day, rather than reaching a specific goal or end point.

On our life journeys, people's sense of Purpose can either remain
constant or change over time, and this varies based on individual experiences, beliefs, and life situations. As you go through different stages of

life and encounter various circumstances, your understanding of your Purpose can evolve and adapt. This means your Purpose can grow and shift along with your personal growth and changes in your life.

What is constant though is that true Purpose is inherently tied to being of Service to others. This service can manifest in countless ways, whether it's to an individual, family, team, company, community, country, or even the world at large. The sphere and manner in which one chooses to serve are deeply personal and vary greatly from person to person. There is no right or wrong way to choose to be of service; it is as unique to you as a fingerprint. Being a great parent or partner or neighbor can be enough—and for many people it is. It's a wonderful and honorable way to live a life of Purpose.

But many people seek to find their Purpose in their work and careers—and this is who we wrote this book for.

Whatever the distinct combination that adds up to your Purpose, everything we've seen and researched on the topic shows that it has the potential to give anyone a sense of clarity, courage, and focus that has tremendous benefits, as we share later on in this section.

But first let's talk about a common phenomenon that we've seen in many people who have desired to go on a quest for Purpose—a *crucible moment.*

CRUCIBLE MOMENTS: THE CATALYSTS FOR SEEKING PURPOSE

Any study of Purpose must include a profound book called *Man's Search for Meaning* by Viktor Frankl, written in 1959.

Frankl was a prisoner in Nazi concentration camps in World War II. He noticed something in the middle of all that tragedy and terror—that those who had a reason to survive beyond themselves were the ones who developed the most resilience and were the ones most likely to survive.

He put it beautifully in this quote by Friedrich Nietzsche that features prominently in the book: "Those who have a 'why' to live can bear almost any 'how.'"

Frankl's experience speaks to something we have noticed in countless people we have interviewed about finding Purpose—that oftentimes it starts with what is called a *crucible moment*: a transformative experience through which an individual comes to a new or an altered sense of identity.

This could be a life-changing, world-altering moment where your world turns upside down. For some people, it can a revelatory moment that profoundly transforms us. For Bobby, it was seeing his son for the first time.

For others, it could be rooted in trauma, such as a near-death experience, someone close to you dying, a natural disaster, or a catastrophic financial event. For Afdhel, one of those early moments was being in his native Sri Lanka in 2004 and miraculously escaping being caught in the massive tsunami that struck the country.

It caused a crack in his universe: he suffered from major post-traumatic stress disorder, in the form known as survivor's guilt.

It led him to reflect on his journey through life and what he was contributing as a marketer and a business leader.

It was certainly one of the moments where the seed was planted in his head: "Why did I survive, and what am I supposed to do with my time on this planet?"

That led him many years later at another crucible moment—when he became a father himself—to go on the journey with Bobby and write their first book.

RECOGNIZING YOUR OWN CRUCIBLE MOMENT

Many of you reading this book may have gone through your own crucible moments.

Certainly, the COVID-19 pandemic was one such universal crucible moment: it left so many of us asking the similar questions about our Purpose—which is why we wrote this book for you.

If you survived it, if you were blessed with resiliency that allowed you to make it through that moment (and so many unfortunately didn't), then life has given you a gift: a gift of time, of potential, and of opportunity.

You may have a nagging sense that there is something more to life than just climbing a career ladder at work.

Feeling that there's more to life than just advancing in your career can be a sign that you're entering a new stage of personal growth. This concept aligns well with Adam Grant's insightful quote about the three stages of self-esteem in a career, which encapsulates this transition beautifully:

Stage 1: I'm not important

Stage 2: I *am* important

Stage 3: I want to *work on* something important

For so many of us, Stage 3 is now happening earlier and earlier in our careers.

Whatever your journey to this moment of self-awareness is, whatever your crucible moment, if you are reading this book right now, you may be wondering whether there is something else you are meant to do with your life next.

And for us, the answer is clear: yes, there is.

And it turns out that finding your Purpose has tremendous transformative power—for all of us, as leaders and employees, in the form of better mental, physical, and spiritual outcomes.

The evolution of self-esteem in a career:

Stage 1: I'm not important

Stage 2: I *am* important

Stage 3: I want to *work on* something important

—Adam Grant, author and professor

CHAPTER 6

THE BENEFITS OF HAVING A PERSONAL PURPOSE

> Having a Purpose is the difference between making a living
> and making a life.
> —Tom Thiss, American author

The more we started to research the benefits of Purpose, the more we found data that made our jaws drop.

Across pretty much every aspect of human existence, from physical and mental outcomes to career success, having a deep sense of Purpose has incredible benefits. We explore those in this chapter.

PHYSICAL HEALTH

Let's start with physical health: something so many of us struggle with. Emerging studies increasingly link a heightened sense of Purpose to a spectrum of favorable outcomes (Kim et al. 2022).

These encompass an array of health behaviors such as enhanced physical activity, greater engagement in preventive health care practices, improved sleep hygiene, and diminished instances of substance misuse.

Moreover, individuals with a stronger sense of Purpose often exhibit superior biological functioning, marked by reduced allostatic load and inflammation levels.

This translates into enhanced physical capabilities and a lowered susceptibility to various ailments, including but not limited to cardiovascular disease and cognitive decline, ultimately contributing to a longer lifespan.

Purpose is a secret force that can help unlock a life of vitality, resilience, and flourishing.

PURPOSE AND MENTAL WELL-BEING

It's not just physical health that Purpose helps with—it's mental health too!

For example, having greater Purpose in life is significantly associated with lower levels of depression and anxiety (Boreham and Schutte 2023).

Other research also indicates that Purpose in life may build greater resilience after exposure to negative events (Schaefer et al. 2013).

Remember Nietzsche's quote? "He who has a 'why' to live can bear almost any 'how.'"

All of these physical and mental benefits make it clear why Purpose is such a powerful thing to find. This may be why so many of us are clamoring to find it in the place where for centuries it was missing—in our work and careers.

PURPOSE AND NEW EXPECTATIONS OF WORK

We believe that there has now been a massive societal shift in expectations around Purpose and work. The desire for a job to give employees Purpose (not just a paycheck) is the new normal.

We believe that there is now an expectation that work—the place we spend eight hours a day, five days a week, 40 years of our life—*should* be a source of meaning too.

And by the way, this wasn't just the expectations of younger generations such as millennials and Gen Z. This was a desire that cut across all generations of people in the workforce, including Gen Xers and baby boomers.

We came across the data in the following graphic before COVID-19 hit.

Millennials and older workers have many of the same career goals

	Millennials	Gen X	Baby Boomers
Make a positive impact on my organization	25%	21%	23%
Help solve social and/or environmental challenges	22%	20%	24%
Work with a diverse group of people	22%	22%	21%
Work for an organization among the best in my industry	21%	25%	23%
Do work I am passionate about	20%	21%	23%
Become an expert in my field	20%	20%	15%
Manage my work-life balance	18%	22%	21%
Become a senior leader	18%	18%	18%
Achieve financial security	17%	16%	18%
Start my own business	17%	12%	15%

Source: IBM's Institute for Business Value released a report titled "Myths, Exaggerations and Uncomfortable Truths: The Real Story Behind Millennials in the Workplace."

When asked the question "What are the most important goals for your work," the first answer was obvious: "I want to make a positive impact on my organization." Who wouldn't?

But look at number two.

"I want to help solve social and/or environmental challenges."

People are telling leaders in companies that they are hungry for meaning.

They want their work to ladder up to something more than just a sales target or a quarterly profit goal.

They want to look back at the legacy of their careers and feel that the work they did mattered—that they contributed to leaving the world better than they found it.

And to us this gives hope.

If we truly are to unleash the enormous potential of business to become a force for good in the world, then the only way to do it is by meeting the equally enormous desire among employees to work on something important and leave this world better than we found it.

It's clear that employees of all generations are questioning why they work beyond a paycheck—and the sad reality is that there is a massive disconnect between what they want and how they feel their organizations treat them.

In the tumult of the recent past, a seismic shift unfolded, propelling the elevation of personal Purpose and values. According to Gartner (2023), a resounding 82% of employees underscore the significance of being recognized by their organizations as individuals, not mere cogs in the corporate machine. However, a sobering reality dawns as only 45% of employees feel their organizations genuinely perceive them through this lens.

So, as you consider your journey to Purpose at work, know that you are not alone: these new expectations around "Purpose, not just a paycheck" being a new normal are part of a radical shift in the way people see work.

WHEN SHOULD YOU START YOUR JOURNEY?

A question we get asked all the time is "Am I ready to go on a journey to find personal Purpose?"

Some of you at the beginning of your career may feel that there are other more immediate priorities.

Sometimes it's also about making sure you are operating from a place of safety and security. For those of us struggling to make our rent, to pay for our children's food or health insurance, finding Purpose may simply be a luxury that is too hard to achieve right now.

And that is okay. It's important to only go on this journey when you are ready and not force it.

But here's one quick story we love, which shows you how Purpose can be accessible to anyone, at any stage of their journey. It's the story of President John F. Kennedy walking around NASA in the 1960s, after he had issued his famous challenge to go to the moon.

In the story, he sees a janitor mopping the floor and walks up to him. Engaging him in conversation, he asks the simple question, "What do you do here?"

The janitor stood straight up, looked the president in the eye, and said, "Mr. President, I'm here to put a man on the moon."

That story shows how no matter how humble the task, no matter what position they occupy, or what title they have, *everyone* can reframe what they do to focus on the higher-order Purpose of the organization.

We may not have choices in how the world sees us.

We may not have choices in what opportunities are open to us.

But we always have a choice in how we see ourselves—and how we frame our worth.

"EVERYBODY CAN BE GREAT BECAUSE EVERYBODY CAN SERVE. YOU DON'T HAVE TO HAVE A COLLEGE DEGREE TO SERVE. YOU DON'T HAVE TO MAKE YOUR SUBJECT AND YOUR VERB AGREE TO SERVE. YOU ONLY NEED A HEART FULL OF GRACE, A SOUL GENERATED BY LOVE."

—Martin Luther King Jr., American minister and civil rights activist

THE BENEFITS OF PURPOSE TO EMPLOYERS

In this section, we look at the enormous benefits of Purpose to employers. Let's start with a staggering fact we found early in our research. According to a Gallup global survey, only 23% of employees reported feeling engaged at work.

Twenty-three percent!

That means that 77% of employees are disengaged at work. Gallup called this "a shocking waste of talent," and we agree.

We think about all those employees out there who are dissatisfied with their work, watching the clock and counting the minutes until they can get home . . . and how much more potential could be unleashed if we could find a way to help them "get in alignment with their assignment" and find a deep sense of meaning and Purpose in what they do.

(Note: while that number went up to 33% for the United States and Canada, that still leaves two-thirds of workers not engaged [Gallup 2023].)

Benefits of Purpose to employers:

- 57% lower employee turnover
- 90% engagement level in Purpose-driven companies
- 225% more productive

(*Sources*: Benevity 2018, Garton and Mankins 2015)

It turns out that there are many good reasons why employers should encourage their employees to find their personal Purpose and explore ways to connect them to the Purpose of their companies.

Attracting Talent

First, let's talk about attracting talent. Let's look at what happened after two years of the COVID-19 pandemic.

The desire for Purpose and meaning hockey-sticked—again, especially among the millennial and Gen-Z groups.

In a recent survey, a compelling 63% of millennials—the dynamic workforce under 35, accounting for over one-third of the US workplace population—voiced a perspective that transcends traditional business paradigms. For them, the core Purpose of businesses should pivot toward "improving society" rather than the conventional mantra of "generating profit" (Goleman n.d.).

Delving deeper, a comprehensive study by the Society for Human Resource Management unveils an even more resolute sentiment: a staggering 94% of millennials are driven by the desire to deploy their skills as a force for good, aiming to contribute meaningfully to a cause (Gurchiek 2014).

And when it comes to the cohort that's following millennials into the workforce, again the data is even more compelling. Born between 1997 and 2012, Generation Z—or Gen Z—currently make up 30% of the world's population and are expected to account for 27% of the workforce by 2025.

This newest generation emphasizes Purpose over pay, meticulously assessing mission statements and values to align with their own. They demand authenticity and transparency, readily calling out inconsistencies, especially regarding environmental or social impacts. Companies veering from ethical practices risk losing these individuals, who prioritize integrity and a positive workplace culture over mere profits.

So the implications are clear: if you want to attract the best talent from the biggest two generations in your workforce, current and future, you need to make sure you can authentically and clearly show how the work they are doing matters.

"THOSE WHO ARE VALUED GET TO CREATE VALUE."

—Nilofer Merchant, author and cofounder, Intangible Labs

Retaining Talent

Next, let's talk about retention.

A study by employee engagement technology company Benevity showed that companies that engage their employees in activities that help their Purpose flourish—even simply through things such as volunteering or matching funds—lead to a 57% lower turnover rate (Benevity 2018).

This is huge because the cost of replacing an employee who leaves is approximately 1.5–2 times their annual salary, which for US-based companies totals more than a staggering trillion dollars a year (Gallup 2019).

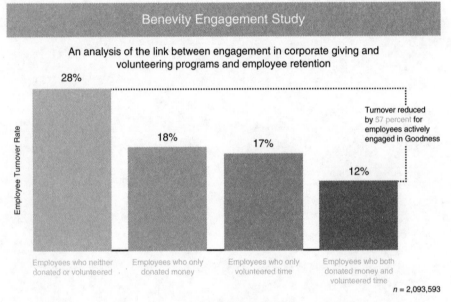

Source: https://www.gallup.com/workplace/247391/fixable-problem-costs-businesses-trillion.aspx

Secondly, remember that Gallup poll showing how low employee engagement was? Well, it turns out that in Purpose-driven companies, engagement is on average 63% versus 31% at other companies (Blount and Leinwand 2019).

According to research from Bain and Company and the *Economist,* Purpose-driven employees are 225% more productive! (Garton and Mankins 2015).

And Deloitte found that Purpose-driven companies are 30% more innovative (O'Brien et al. 2019).

Growth and Profitability

All of which ladders up to the holy grail of all businesses: profit. The data shows that more than 90% of Purpose-driven companies deliver growth and profits at or above industry average (Blount and Leinwand 2019).

And Korn Ferry's study showed that Purpose-driven companies posted compounded annual growth rates of 9.85% compared to 2.4% for the whole S&P 500 Consumer Sector (Feldman n.d.).

Beyond the data, we see this every day in our work at Conspiracy of Love, working with C-suite leaders in some of the biggest companies on the planet such as Sephora, Coca-Cola, and The Gap.

Those wise leaders recognize that Purpose is the secret weapon that can help them attract and retain talent and unleash tremendous energy, innovation, and growth inside their walls.

"CREATE THE ROLE YOU LOVE . . . FIND WHERE YOU SPARKLE WITHIN OUR ORGANIZATION AND TOGETHER LET'S FIND A WAY FOR YOU TO DO MORE OF THAT, WHILE SERVING OUR **PURPOSE."**

—Alicia Kennedy, writer

THE BENEFITS OF PURPOSE TO EMPLOYEES

Next, let's look at the benefits of Purpose to employees.

It turns out having clarity about your personal Purpose—and finding work in a company whose Purpose and values align with yours—has tremendous benefits.

Let's start with income and net worth. Studies show that Purpose-driven employees often find themselves on a trajectory to higher incomes and enhanced net worth (Hill et al. 2016).

For instance, they are 10% more likely to have received a raise in the last 12 months (BetterUp 2018). This may be because having a sense of Purpose leads to 64% higher levels of fulfillment. And that's not all—it turns out that Purpose-driven employees are 50% more likely to achieve leadership positions (Hurst et al. 2016).

See why we think this is such a powerful topic for all employees to explore?

Benefits of a Purpose-driven career to employees:

- Five times higher levels of well-being
- Four times higher levels of engagement
- 50% higher likelihood of being in leadership

(Source: Imperative, Hurst et al. 2016)

"WHEN YOU ARE DECID- ING ON NEXT STEPS, NEXT JOBS, NEXT CAREERS, FURTHER EDUCATION, YOU SHOULD RATHER FIND PURPOSE THAN A JOB OR A CAREER. PURPOSE CROSSES DISCIPLINES. PURPOSE IS AN ESSENTIAL ELEMENT OF YOU."

—Chadwick Boseman, actor

PURPOSE AND LEADERS: THE BENEFITS

Finally, let's look at the benefits of Purpose to leaders.

It turns out that, according to the *Harvard Business Review*, Purpose-driven leaders cultivate environments where satisfaction, engagement, and retention flourish. Their employees stand 70% more satisfied, 56% more engaged, and an impressive 100% more likely to stay with the organization (Urban Land Institute 2014).

When it comes to effectiveness, according to research from the University of Notre Dame, Purpose-driven leaders emerge with a leadership effectiveness score soaring 63% higher than their reactive counterparts (Anderson and Adams 2015).

And, according to research by EY, 75% of executives at Purpose-driven companies report that the integration of Purpose creates value in the short term, as well as over the long run. Having a well-integrated Purpose helps their company navigate disruption, according to 73% of business leaders.

In these volatile and turbulent times, Purpose can be the force that helps leaders keep their teams motivated and focused.

In the dynamic landscape of leadership, Purpose emerges not merely as a guiding force but as the linchpin that propels individuals into positions of influence and effectiveness. As we unravel the correlation between Purpose and leadership, a compelling narrative of empowerment and satisfaction unfolds.

A WATCHOUT

But there is a big disconnect between managers and frontline employees.

According to research by McKinsey, only 15% of frontline employees said they were living their Purpose at work, versus 85% of executives and upper management.

Left unchecked, this can simmer into discontent and boil over into open revolt.

It's something we advise our clients to keep an eye open for all the time. This *Purpose gulf* can lead to everything from employee gripes aired on Slack channels to confrontations at town halls—and even walkouts and strikes, as we have seen in many companies from Activision to Adidas.

Good leaders should take the time to ensure that Purpose is accessible and encouraged to everyone at every level in their organizations—and ensure that the conditions for it to flourish are constantly nurtured.

"PEOPLE WANT TO WORK FOR SOME PURPOSE BIGGER THAN THEMSELVES. THAT MAKES A DIFFERENCE BETWEEN GOOD AND GREAT WORK."

—Tim Cook, Apple CEO

CHAPTER 7

THE NINE TRUTHS OF PURPOSE

> Efforts and courage are not enough without Purpose
> and direction.
> —John F. Kennedy, 35th US President

Hopefully, the data in Chapter 6 helped reassure you that there are strong scientific correlations between Purpose and physical, mental, and financial benefits—and showed leaders the benefits of creating a safe, inclusive, and Purpose-driven environment.

So let's get to the good stuff! How should you think about this complex topic?

We've broken it down into nine truths that our years of research and practice have revealed.

1. Purpose is a direction, not a destination.
2. Purpose is a river with many streams.
3. Purpose is about getting in alignment with your assignment.
4. Purpose is about self-transcendence.
5. Purpose is what makes you feel alive.
6. Purpose is about what puts you in a flow state.
7. Purpose is about operating in your zone of genius.
8. Purpose is about unleashing your inner intrapreneur.
9. Purpose is about using your moral imagination.

1. PURPOSE IS A DIRECTION, NOT A DESTINATION

Let's start with the first truth: *Purpose is a direction, not a destination.*

For some people it may seem as if their Purpose stays consistent throughout their life, but the expressions of it change. For others, it may seem that there are different Purposes for different stages of their lives.

Either way, it's important to think about Purpose as a dynamic, living, breathing thing that you should pay attention to.

Instead of asking the question, "What do I want to do for the *rest* of my life" (which comes with such pressure!), ask, "What do I feel drawn to explore more deeply at this *moment* in my life?"

This allows you to constantly keep calibrating and making changes to ensure you stay on track.

What's important is the direction you are heading in—as opposed to one final destination that is your "Purpose" for eternity.

2. PURPOSE IS A RIVER
WITH MANY STREAMS

Here's another reality about Purpose: its sources are manifold and unique to each person, like a mighty river fed by many streams flowing into it from different sources.

Let's try this exercise for a second:

Think about the places where you find meaning in your life.

Purpose is about a sense of direction or a calling to strive toward (a North Star).

Meaning is more about understanding and significance.

Purpose and meaning are both crucial for a fulfilling and satisfying life, and they often influence and reinforce each other. For example, pursuing a purposeful goal (such as a career or a personal project) can provide a sense of meaning, and having a deep sense of meaning in your life can help you identify or affirm your Purpose.

Everyone has different sources of meaning and Purpose in their lives.

For many people, it could be their family: We certainly know the deep sense of meaning that we get from being good fathers and husbands.

Becoming a parent is a moment when you realize that you are responsible for a life that is not your own. Navigating the struggles and challenges of parenting can be especially rewarding and meaningful.

Faith is another deep source of meaning for many: your belief in a religion or a higher power can be something that gives you solace in times of trouble, and spirituality can be a way of making sense of the complex and confusing world we live in.

For others, it maybe their country and patriotism that gives them a sense of meaning: think about soldiers who volunteer to give up their

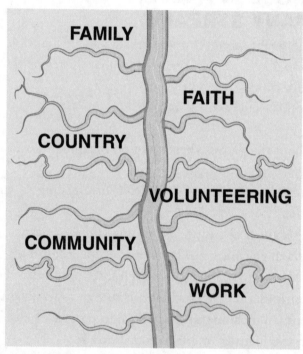

Purpose is a river with many streams.

lives in order to protect their nation, or people who work in government to try to make the lives of their fellow citizens better.

Or it could be something more close at hand, such as being part of a community: whether it's your neighborhood block association, your child's school association, or a local sports team—that shared sense of being part of something bigger, of helping make your community better can be a deep source of meaning.

Or it could be volunteering or fundraising for a cause that is close to your heart: Bobby is still deeply involved in Peace First because the idea of "feeding the good" in young people is ingrained in his heart. Afdhel is on the board of Choose Love, a charity involved in helping refugees and displaced people around the world.

In fact, the one place that *isn't* supposed to have meaning is your job. A job is just a job, right? A place to go and work and collect your paycheck.

(There is still a proportion of folks out there who believe this. If you are in this segment, keep reading! This book may help you see your work differently.)

In fact, those who found meaning in their job were said to have found their *calling* (in fact, the word 'vocation' comes from the latin 'vocare' meaning 'calling').

But we think this is what is changing in the world. Employees no longer want to wait until they retire to give back.

Especially for younger generations who lived through the 2008 financial crisis and saw their parents' house, 401(k), life savings, and confidence decimated, there is a new expectation. They want their work to matter *now*, not at some future abstract point in their lives.

If you are in this cohort of people, that's probably why you are reading this book.

3. PURPOSE IS ABOUT GETTING IN ALIGNMENT WITH YOUR ASSIGNMENT

We believe the universal truth that Purpose is about finding ways to be of service through your work.

Some of us may be lucky enough to already work at a Purpose-driven organization where the overlap and connection between the Purpose of the company and our personal Purpose is clear and strong.

For others, it may require going on a journey to find a place of work that feels more in sync with your values and beliefs.

Our friend and Purpose coach Tru Pettigrew coined the phrase "Getting in alignment with your assignment" and it's an idea we love.

What we interpret that to mean is finding ways to first understand what our personal Purpose is (this is where your personal GPS comes in, which you'll work on in Part 3 of this book) and then seeking ways to explore that at work.

For instance, your GPS may show a Passion around mental health. There may be small steps you can take to start investigating right there in the company you are already working for.

Perhaps that is something you could explore via your company's volunteering program—taking some time to find nonprofits in your community that you could volunteer with to feed your curiosity about the topic—and see if this is something you want to contribute more to.

This may lead you to joining an ERG (Employee Resource Group) that celebrates positive mental well-being—or even getting support from your employer to set one up if one doesn't exist.

You might discover a deep Passion around the issue of inclusivity. Again, this might take the form of joining internal groups focused on progressing DEI inside your company.

It may seem alien to you at first: after all, a lot of us are taught to put on a corporate facade that separates work from life and to keep parts of your life hidden.

But understanding the parts of yourself that are authentic to you and their corresponding areas of interest is the first step to going on that journey.

You may be surprised what you find!

4. PURPOSE IS ABOUT SELF-TRANSCENDENCE

At some point in your life—maybe in high school, maybe in a college undergraduate course—you have probably seen this diagram.

It's pretty famous.

Abraham Maslow was an American psychologist who in 1943 created this hierarchy of needs based on what he believed to be the criteria for achieving psychological health.

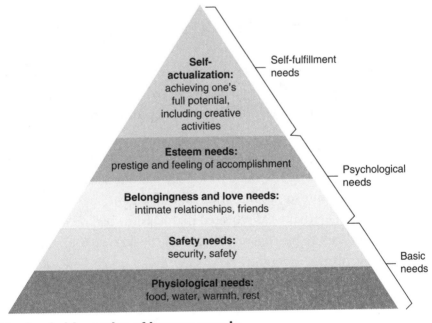

Self-actualization: achieving one's full potential, including creative activities

Self-fulfillment needs

Esteem needs: prestige and feeling of accomplishment

Belongingness and love needs: intimate relationships, friends

Psychological needs

Safety needs: security, safety

Physiological needs: food, water, warmth, rest

Basic needs

Maslow's hierarchy of human needs.

The needs are ranked in ascending priority: from the most basic needs at the bottom to the highest-order needs at the top.

At the very bottom are *physiological needs,* such as food, water, warmth, and rest. Without these needs being satisfied, it's impossible to move up the ladder.

Next come *safety needs,* such as security and stability. Think about someone who is homeless and living on the streets and how that creates such a rocky, uncertain place to live life from.

Then come *belongingness and love needs*—intimate relationships with partners or a friend group. Think about how having these things helps our sense of well-being and security.

Then come *esteem needs*—defined as "prestige and feelings of accomplishment." For instance, how does your job title make you feel? Does it help you communicate your level of achievement to the world and how you have advanced?

At the very top of the pyramid, Maslow put *self-actualization,* which he defined as "achieving one's full potential, including creative activities."

Now here comes the interesting part: as Bobby and I went on our parallel journeys through corporate life, we achieved all of these levels, in different ways. But when we got to the top of the pyramid, we still felt empty inside.

And we were not alone: Many of the leaders we interviewed along the way reported feeling the same way. They had the salary, the title, the teams, the power. But something was still missing.

It was only then that we discovered that Maslow had *changed* the top of the pyramid before he died in 1970, in a little-known journal.

The top of the pyramid now says *self-transcendence,* not *self-actualization.*

This is where the pyramid stops being about you and starts being about how you transcend *yourself*. In other words, it's about how you become of service to the world. (A topic we're going to dive into much deeper later in the book.)

Maslow had realized that focusing the pyramid narrowly on the self was egotistical and ultimately not something that gave people long-term satisfaction.

By turning the attention outward—by reversing the polarity—paradoxically it brings a tremendous amount of satisfaction inwards. Self-transcendence, in its essence, invites us to ascend beyond the confines of the self, establishing a profound connection with something larger, something grander.

It's the recognition that we are mere fragments in the mosaic of a greater whole and, in response, navigating our actions with this cosmic awareness in mind.

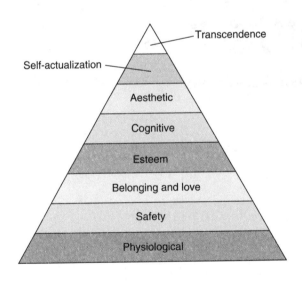

"WE MAKE A LIVING BY WHAT WE GET, BUT WE MAKE A LIFE BY WHAT WE GIVE."

—Winston Churchill

5. PURPOSE IS WHAT MAKES YOU FEEL ALIVE

In the wisdom of Maslow, the concept of self-transcendence unfolds as a gateway to what he eloquently dubbed "peak experiences." Within these transformative moments, individuals ascend beyond their personal concerns, attaining a vantage point of higher perspective. Invariably, these encounters usher in a tapestry of potent positive emotions—joy, peace, and a finely tuned awareness that resonates on a profound level.

Here's how Maslow defined peak experiences:

> Feelings of limitless horizons opening up to the vision, the feeling of being simultaneously more powerful and also more helpless than one ever was before, the feeling of great ecstasy and wonder and awe, the loss of placing in time and space with, finally, the conviction that something extremely important and valuable had happened, so that the subject is to some extent transformed and strengthened even in his daily life by such experiences.

How do you find these peak experiences? A good clue is finding those things that make you come alive.

Howard Thurman was a luminary of American history, donning various hats—author, philosopher, theologian, mystic, educator, and civil rights leader. His indelible mark on the canvas of social justice movements and organizations during the 20th century positions him as a guiding force within the spiritual realm and a key influencer in the ebb and flow of societal change.

He summed this idea up beautifully in this quote:

> Don't ask yourself what the world needs. Ask yourself what makes you come alive, and go do that, because what the world needs is people who have come alive (Thurman 2010).

"DON'T ASK WHAT THE WORLD NEEDS. ASK WHAT BRINGS YOU ALIVE. BECAUSE WHAT THE WORLD NEEDS IS PEOPLE WHO HAVE COME ALIVE."

—Howard Thurman, American author and philosopher

Think about what brings you alive. Think about what brings you energy and doesn't deplete you.

For everyone, these things are different.

For some, it could be their family or faith, their community or country. It could be parts of their work. For instance, some people get great satisfaction in helping a teammate learn something new, by coaching and mentoring them.

For others, it could be being the one who has a breakthrough idea that can help innovate a new product or service or even transform what a company does.

Take a few minutes to write these down.

THINGS THAT BRING ME ENERGY

6. PURPOSE IS ABOUT WHAT PUTS YOU IN A FLOW STATE

Here's another clue: does it put you in a flow state?

A *flow state*, akin to a symphony of focused cognition, unfolds when an individual is completely immersed in a task or activity. Within this state, the mind becomes a singular force, free from the clutter of self-reflection or performance evaluation.

In the realm of flow, certain hallmarks emerge:

- A profound sense of accomplishment, as if one has conquered the task at hand.
- The activity acquires a heightened sense of meaningfulness, transcending the mundane.
- Positive mood states permeate the consciousness, creating an uplifting atmosphere.
- Calmness prevails, serenading the individual with a tranquil mental backdrop.
- Self-consciousness takes a backseat, allowing undistracted engagement with the task.
- Anxiety retreats, granting a serene space for focused creativity.
- Senses become heightened, attuned to the nuances of the present moment.
- Time seems to slow down, elongating the perception of each passing moment.

These characteristics articulate the experience of flow, a beautiful state where the individual and the activity harmonize into a seamless unity.

What puts you into a flow state is different for everyone, and there is no right or wrong answer. But doing work that triggers this state more often than not is a great clue that you are doing something that is meaningful, when time slips away and you can access something deeper in yourself.

Take some time to think about specific things that put you in a flow state.

THINGS THAT PUT ME IN A FLOW STATE

7. PURPOSE IS ABOUT OPERATING IN YOUR ZONE OF GENIUS

Here's another great way to think about your Purpose: Does it allow you to operate primarily in your *zone of genius?*

This is where you are operating at your fullest potential, doing something that only you can do or that you are the best you know at doing it.

The Big Leap, penned by the insightful Gay Hendricks (2010), a luminary in psychology and personal development, stands as a road map for unraveling and transcending the self-imposed constraints that act as barriers to individuals realizing their boundless potential.

Within the pages of this guide, Hendricks intricately navigates the landscape of human limitations, offering profound insights that pave the way for genuine happiness and unparalleled success. It's not just a book; it's a transformative journey toward unleashing one's fullest potential and basking in the radiance of authentic joy and accomplishment.

We highly recommend you read it! But if you don't have time, here's one of the core ideas expressed in the book. His theory is that all of us operate in four zones of competence:

- **The zone of incompetence:** A terrain where we find ourselves entangled in tasks that elude our proficiency, squandering precious time and energy on endeavors that offer little to no return.
- **The zone of competence:** Here, we navigate through tasks that fall within our capabilities but lack the spark of joy or fulfillment. These are duties undertaken not out of Passion but out of sheer ability.
- **The zone of excellence:** Many find themselves comfortably situated in this zone, basking in recognition and rewards for their adeptness. However, despite the external accolades, there's a lingering sense of unfulfillment—a space where proficiency doesn't necessarily align with Passion.

- **The zone of genius:** Ah, the apex of potential! The zone of genius is where our authentic selves shine. It's the realm of our unique abilities and Passions, where work feels truly fulfilling. In this zone, we're not just good; we're in our element, feeling alive, and authentically ourselves.

There is huge potential in reorganizing our lives toward spending as much time as possible in the zone of genius. It's not just about excellence; it's about aligning with our true Purpose, where Gifts, Passions and Service converge to craft a life rich in fulfillment.

So spend some time thinking about your zones of genius.

WHEN AM I OPERATING IN MY ZONE OF GENIUS?

8. PURPOSE IS ABOUT UNLEASHING YOUR INNER INTRAPRENEUR

Now we come to one of our favorite topics: helping explain the concept of an *intrapreneur*.

This is for those of you who may have already dabbled in finding ways to bring your Purpose to life—such as joining an Employee Resource Group (ERG) or volunteering with your company—and want to go even further.

While an entrepreneur is someone who decides to start their own business, an *intrapreneur* is a person who decides to act entrepreneurially within the context of an existing business—oftentimes, in Service of solving a societal or environmental problem.

Intrapreneurs embody a distinctive breed of employees—driven, proactive, and fueled by a relentless desire to pioneer innovative products or services within their organizational confines.

Coined by none other than Steve Jobs in 1985, the word *intrapreneur* seamlessly blends "internal" and "entrepreneur," encapsulating the essence of these corporate trailblazers. They don't merely wait for opportunities; they forge them.

Picture this: self-starters who harbor both ambition and a laser-focused pursuit of goals. With an innate ability to tackle challenges independently, intrapreneurs aren't just problem solvers; they're architects of process enhancements. They thrive in self-assumed roles, even venturing into unfamiliar territory, driven by a hunger for new challenges.

In the realm of intrapreneurship, these individuals are not just employees; they are catalysts of innovation, weaving a narrative of proactive determination and a penchant for transformative risk-taking within the corporate landscape.

In fact, there is an entire international organization dedicated to supporting and inspiring intrapreneurs in many different companies—it's called *The League of Intrapreneurs*, and it was started by a woman we admire tremendously called Maggie De Pree (Check out www.league ofintrapreneurs.com for more info).

Bobby and I wish we had known about this concept and this amazing organization while we were still in corporate life.

For a long time in our careers, even though we were working for great companies with wonderful colleagues on interesting projects, we struggled with finding meaning and fulfillment in the work we were doing.

We kept trying to "smuggle in" more purposeful projects in the work we were doing, creating partnerships with nonprofits and trying to find ways to grow the brands we were working on in ways that were socially, financially, and culturally powerful.

Without knowing it, we were trying to be "social intrapreneurs."

In our previous two books—*The Good Is the New Cool Guide to Meaningful Marketing* and *The Good Is the New Cool Guide to Conscious Business*—we interviewed many different inspiring social intrapreneurs, such as Saul Dave at Zappos, who helped the retail giant set up a multimillion-dollar new business unit around adaptive clothing for disabled people, and Saqib Shaikh at Microsoft, who invented a new technology called Seeing AI to help blind people see the world using the power of artificial intelligence.

We've also interviewed so many of them for our 'Good Is the New Cool' podcast series, which you can check out at anywhere you listen to your podcasts.

This is the work we get to do with our consultancy Conspiracy of Love—by going into some of the biggest companies on the planet such as Coca-Cola, Adidas, and Sephora and helping unleash the intrapreneurs who can help the company grow in a new way, essentially "positively disrupting" them from the inside.

It may mean realizing that your own life experience—for instance, as a member of a minority or marginalized group—could be of tremendous value to your company as it looks to what we call *inclusive growth*—finding new ways to grow your company by reaching new consumers with innovative products and services that cater to their needs.

Later in this book, we're going to introduce you to three inspiring intrapreneurs to illuminate how they used their Gifts and Passions to be of Service—Lindsey Roy from Hallmark, Aaron Mitchell from Netflix, and Kim Culmone from Mattel (who was behind Barbie's amazing reinvention into the cultural icon she is today).

Take a moment to think about your own career and your own company.

Are there ideas you've had that can help change the world for the better and help your company grow?

MY INTRAPRENEURIAL IDEAS

"PURSUE SOMETHING SO IMPORTANT THAT EVEN IF YOU FAIL, THE WORLD IS BETTER OFF WITH YOU HAVING TRIED."

—Tim O'Reilly, author and CEO

9. PURPOSE IS ABOUT USING YOUR MORAL IMAGINATION

What is moral imagination? Simply put, it's using your imagination to imagine the world as it should be—not as it is.

Think about an injustice in the world you may have noticed or experienced, either in your community or in the workplace. Did it leave you with a burning desire to want to fix the problem so that nobody else had to go through it ever again? Did it spark ideas in your head and your heart about how to find a solution to overcome it?

If so, you are already using your moral imagination. It's a Gift that all of us have but few of us choose to use.

Great leaders throughout history have practiced moral imagination: from Gandhi to Dr. Martin Luther King Jr to Mother Teresa. But we believe that this practice should not just be limited to politics and impact: it can be equally powerful in the world of business as we reimagine a new version that is in service to people and planet.

Embarking on the realm of moral imagination calls for a nuanced perspective—a capacity to conceive innovative paths that intertwine ethics and success seamlessly.

This multifaceted ability involves the orchestration of ideas that can benefit others and the decisive execution of these concepts to extend a helping hand to those who need it.

As explained by the philosopher Mark Johnson, moral imagination goes beyond mere strength of character; it's about envisioning the kaleidoscope of possibilities within a given situation to navigate ethical challenges. It demands a keen sensitivity to people and life situations, coupled with a foresight that contemplates both the potential help and harm stemming from our actions.

Moral imagination emerges as a beacon guiding individuals and businesses to chart a course that transcends the dichotomy of ethics and success. It's a call to peer beyond the balance sheets and consider the profound impact of decisions on the well-being of others.

In essence, moral imagination, when fused with creativity and moral courage, becomes the catalyst propelling individuals and businesses toward more ethically grounded actions within society. At its best, it is a transformative force that sparks positive change.

A SIDEBAR STORY: PRACTICE CATHEDRAL THINKING

Maybe you're familiar with the tale of Christopher Wren, the eminent English architect.

Once, he strolled incognito among the laborers constructing St. Paul's Cathedral in London, a structure he had designed.

Curious, he asked one worker, "What are you doing?" The man replied, "I am cutting a piece of stone."

A similar question to another worker yielded a different response: "I am earning five shillings, two pence a day."

However, when posed to a third worker, the reply was, "I am helping Sir Christopher Wren build a beautiful cathedral."

This third individual possessed vision, seeing beyond immediate tasks or daily earnings to contribute to the creation of a magnificent work of art—the construction of a grand cathedral.

Likewise, it is crucial in your life to aspire to perceive the broader and more meaningful perspective.

What is the cathedral you can help build that can exist long beyond your lifespan?

MY MORAL IMAGINATION IDEAS

PART III

YOUR GPS TO PURPOSE

This part of the book helps you find your Purpose. It starts with helping you find a vision of where you want to go in life and then using your Gifts and Passions to Serve the world to get there.

CHAPTER 8

WHAT IS GPS TO PURPOSE?

> When you know your why, you'll never lose your way.
> —Ibukun Ibraheem, innovator and business leader

GPS *to Purpose* is like having a personal navigation system for your life and career. Just as GPS technology guides you from your current location to your desired destination, GPS to Purpose helps you steer your life in a Purpose driven way. Instead of relying on external satellites, this journey taps into the natural guide that resides within us.

Imagine embarking on a road trip to an unfamiliar destination. You'd likely trust your GPS to chart the course and provide directions. Similarly, in the quest for Purpose, we have three internal tools at our disposal.

- First, there are our *Gifts* (G), representing our innate talents, superpowers, and unique qualities. These Gifts are the tools and traits that make us exceptional and valuable in the world.
- Next, we have our *Passions* (P), which illuminate the activities and pursuits that energize us and bring us to life in profound ways.
- The third tool is *Service* (S), which guides us in applying our Gifts and Passions to serve the world around us. It identifies the role we can play in making a positive impact on others.

When we harmonize these elements—our Gifts, Passions, and Service—we begin to move toward a life where we can channel our time into activities that truly energize us, all while serving the needs of others. These components come together to form a personal Purpose statement, akin to our personal North Star, or our Why. With this Purpose as our guiding light, we navigate our life's journey with clarity.

And with the map of a Living Vision, an inspiring visualization of our life, it will help us know when we've arrived.

WHAT THIS JOURNEY WILL HELP YOU ACHIEVE

GPS to Purpose serves as your trusted guide on the journey to a more fulfilling and purpose-driven life. With its assistance, you'll embark on a transformative exploration of self-discovery and alignment, enabling you to:

- **Uncover your unique Gifts:** GPS to Purpose will help you identify and harness your innate talents, strengths, and abilities. It's about recognizing the exceptional qualities that make you who you are and understanding how you can leverage them to make a meaningful impact.

- **Discover your deepest Passions:** Through this process, you'll gain clarity on what truly ignites your soul and fills you with enthusiasm. You'll pinpoint the activities, interests, and pursuits that bring you joy, fulfillment, and a sense of Purpose.

- **Define your Service role:** GPS to Purpose guides you in exploring how you can use your Gifts and Passions to contribute to the well-being of others and the world at large. It helps you identify the areas where you can make a meaningful difference and leave a positive imprint.

- **Craft your Purpose statement:** As these pieces come together, you'll craft a Purpose statement—a clear and powerful expression of your why. This Purpose statement will serve as your unwavering North Star, providing direction, motivation, and a sense of Purpose in all your endeavors.

- **Stay on course:** Armed with your Purpose statement, you'll never lose your way. GPS to Purpose equips you with a reliable navigation system for life, ensuring that you make choices and decisions that align with your Purpose, leading to a more fulfilling and transcendent existence.

In essence, GPS to Purpose empowers you to chart a course toward a life of greater authenticity, fulfillment, and significance. It's your companion on the journey to discovering and living your true Purpose, ensuring that you navigate life's twists and turns with clarity and purposeful intention.

TO PREPARE FOR YOUR JOURNEY

To embark on your journey of self-discovery and Purpose, it's essential to set the stage for a meaningful exploration. The following five suggestions serve as your compass, guiding you toward a focused and productive experience. From creating a conducive environment to embracing an open mindset, these steps will help you make the most of your Purpose-seeking adventure:

- **Create a focused environment:** Find a quiet space, allocate dedicated time, and eliminate distractions to fully engage in self-reflection.
- **Prepare writing materials:** Have a notebook and pen ready to jot down thoughts and insights during the exercise.
- **Adopt an open mindset:** Approach the exercise with curiosity, leaving judgment behind and embracing the opportunity for self-discovery.
- **Reflect on your life journey:** Spend time considering significant life experiences, moments of joy, and past sources of fulfillment to gain insights into your Purpose.
- **Identify key questions:** Prioritize specific questions such as your talents, Passions, and desired impact to guide your Purpose exploration.
- **Find your "Purpose Posse":** A small group of one to three friends or colleagues who know you best and can help you along your journey by providing perspectives and input.

HOW TO USE THIS PART

As you embark on this journey to explore your own GPS, we thought this metaphor may be helpful for you to keep in mind on how to use this part of the book.

Think about yourself walking through a forest. At first the path you are on is clear. But after a while you realize something—there is no more path.

All around you are trees. There are no clear signs telling you which way to go. What do you need in that moment?

You need a direction to set off in. And to do that, you need a compass.

You need a GPS (the methodology of Gifts, Passions, and Service we are going to help you do in this part of the book). And you need a map to tell you when you've arrived (a Living Vision—we'll get to that in a bit).

Armed with that clarity and courage, you set off in a new direction. The path may be unclear at first. In fact, there may not even be a path. You may need to hack your way through some undergrowth at first. The going may be tough, the ground rocky underfoot.

But you persevere.

The sky starts to darken and night sets in. You need a lantern to light the way. At first it only shows you a small circle of light. But with each step you take, the next step becomes clearer. So you just keep moving.

Along the way, you may meet someone else who is also lost. You realize that their path is the same as yours. And suddenly you are not alone anymore. And the path becomes easier because you have help— and someone you can help. (Luckily, this is what happened to Bobby and Afdhel.)

There may be rocks and obstacles along the way that you need to navigate. But having faith in the direction you are going in gives you courage to keep going. After a while, you arrive at a beautiful clearing in the forest. It has peace and shade and everything you need to sustain and energize you.

Ah, you say. This is where I will make camp. For now, that is. Because the time will come when even that beautiful clearing will start to seem too small. And you will feel the urge to go on another journey, another adventure.

You will need to find a new compass heading again for that stage in your life. The desire to find a new Purpose. And that's okay.

Because this book and GPS will always be with you at whatever your stage of life to help you go on your next adventure of meaning and Purpose.

Are you ready to start your journey of Purpose?

CHAPTER 9

YOUR
LIVING VISION

Don't get so busy making a living that you forget to make a life.
—Dolly Parton, musician and icon

The GPS model discussed in the last chapter starts with a Living Vision, which is a map of where you want to go in life, using your Gifts and Passions to serve the world to get there.

The first step is defining what a life of Purpose, Passion, and prosperity looks like for yourself.

In essence, a Living Vision is a vivid, active, and highly specific picture of your ideal life as you wish to live it now. It serves as both a guide and an inspiration for your daily choices and long-term efforts. Specificity is crucial, so be as clear and almost "photorealistic" as you can—write in Technicolor 4K. Also, make sure you write in the present tense ("I am," not "I will"), which will help make this vision more realistic.

(Note: The Living Vision exercise is something we learned from the coach Kirk Souder, whose practice we have greatly benefited from. You can find out more about his work at www.kirksouder.co.)

Key characteristics of a Living Vision include:

- **Present and future oriented:** While it is about the life you want to experience now, it also includes elements that you're working toward in the near future. It's a blend of immediate aspirations and ongoing goals.
- **Dynamic and adaptable:** A Living Vision is not rigid. It evolves as you grow and as your circumstances change. It adapts to new opportunities, learnings, and challenges.
- **Holistic and comprehensive:** It covers all areas of your life, acknowledging that fulfillment comes from a balance of various facets such as career, relationships, personal growth, health, and hobbies.

- **Reflective of personal values and desires:** It's deeply personal and reflects your unique values, Passions, and desires. It's not what others expect from you but what you truly want for yourself.
- **Inspiring and motivating:** A Living Vision provides motivation and a sense of Purpose. It's a source of inspiration that drives you to take action and make choices aligned with your desired life.
- **Visually and emotionally engaging:** It often involves a clear mental or even physical representation (like a vision board) that makes it easy to visualize and emotionally connect with.

"MANY PERSONS HAVE A WRONG IDEA OF WHAT CONSTITUTES TRUE HAPPINESS. IT IS NOT ATTAINED THROUGH SELF-GRATIFICATION BUT THROUGH FIDELITY TO A WORTHY PURPOSE."

—Helen Keller, American author, political activist, and lecturer

YOUR LIVING VISION EXERCISE

Now, grab a cup of coffee and curl up in your favorite nook. Or take this book with you on vacation and write this while you lie on a beach somewhere.

Write unselfconsciously, freeing yourself of the invisible and unspoken limitations you have placed on your life.

Write as if you were looking back at yourself from 10 years in the future. Think about how far you've come from 10 years ago. The life you're living now may not have seemed possible back then, right? Try to imagine a life that doesn't seem possible right now.

The first step is defining what a life of Purpose, Passion, and prosperity looks like for yourself. In essence, a Living Vision is a vivid and active picture of your ideal life as you wish to live it now, serving as both a guide and an inspiration for your daily choices and long-term efforts.

Here are some prompts to think about when writing yours (as you write, be sure to consider the characteristics of a Living Vision covered earlier in this chapter):

- **Imagine your perfect day:** What would you do from the moment that you woke up to the moment that you fell asleep? How would you allocate your time between all the important things in your life—your health, your family, your spirituality, your creativity, your work?
- **Write about how you want to feel, not things you want to have in your life:** Don't write about the size of your house or the number of cars in your driveway or the size of your bank balance. Write about how you want to feel—what are the emotions you want to be experiencing throughout the day? Is it awe, wonder, joy, inspiration, curiosity, gratitude? Make sure you weave in this language throughout your Living Vision.

- **Dream big:** Don't think about incrementally changing what you already have. Instead think about a vision of a world that seems ridiculously out of reach. It's only by freeing yourself of narrow expectations of how good your life could be that you can reach new heights.

Here are our Living Visions to provide you with an idea of how these pieces come together.

Bobby's Living Vision

I am enjoying a deep, peaceful sleep. There are no worries, stresses, or distractions in my mind. I feel good about what I accomplished the day before. I am compassionate to myself, and thus, I can relax my mind and sleep until my body gently wakes me up. I have no negative imaginings. I wake up filled with gratitude, optimism, and enthusiasm for the day ahead. I feel inspired by the day's infinite possibilities and flow through it with faith and openness. I am connected to the four pillars of my life: love, health, wealth, and self-expression. I enjoy them with perfect harmony. I start the day next to my wife with a prayer of gratitude. I listen and tend to what my spirit needs. I am in no rush; the day will unfold perfectly in due time.

I know that I am living my Purpose. I feel completely at peace, and that is the ultimate success to me. I am proud I have achieved it. I stretch my mind to expand my thinking, and my body is flexible and strong. I spend quality time with my wife and son. I am present and attentive to their needs. We eat, talk, laugh, and enjoy each other's company. I have enough time to support their interests and Passions enthusiastically. I am financially secure from my investments, work, and play, which produce constant income that exceeds all my financial needs. I am overflowing with abundance. I pay enough attention to my finances to ensure they can take care of my family for generations and contribute to the causes

I hold dear. I only do work that aligns with my Passions and Purpose. My work is fun and fulfilling. In many ways, it feels like play. I feel worthy of the success I achieved and thankfully receive it knowing that my miracles, success, love, and peace are all here for me by birthright. And I continuously help others achieve the same, whether by coaching, creating, speaking, or leading. My work makes a difference in the world in a meaningful and visible way. I know for sure that I am making significant contributions to the world in many ways.

I travel internationally for inspiration and as an ambassador and evangelist for the work I do. The places I travel open my mind and heart to the diverse beauty of people and our planet. I honor and respect the places I travel, and wherever I go, I meet people who are part of the *Good Is the New Cool* community, which brings me great pleasure and pride. I make soulful connections wherever I go and can communicate in multiple languages. I work wherever and whenever I want. Wherever I go, I connect with incredible creators for good. They are creating businesses, innovations, and solutions that are changing the world. I feel inspired by them, and they are inspired by me. We have the most uplifting conversations on life, spirituality, and possibilities. I am given and equally give myself recognition and respect as a creator, and I'm always working on exciting things that open my mind and heart and add to my story of impact. I have, and I am, creating offerings that are transforming the world for the better in remarkable and lasting ways. I feel completely at peace from the good I am doing.

I give love freely and fearlessly. I know we are all God's creation, and I see and feed the good in all that I see. I am also able to accept love in all forms, and I feel the power of it. I feel connected to my family and friends. We check on each other regularly, and I prioritize spending time with them. It makes me feel grounded and part of my village. I hold no grudges. I forgive and bless all people the same. I often vacation with my loved ones. I host dream trips for my family and friends, opening their eyes to the beauty of the world. We eat delicious meals, see incredible sights, and enjoy our lives to the fullest. No place seems too far to experience and enjoy. I give love and care to everyone around me when we are together.

My work is a perfect expression of self. I am creating wealth for myself and others. I have built spaces in my community where young people can play and imagine freely, explore new possibilities, and learn skills to set them up for a lifetime of success. I have established community spaces for creators to come together to connect, learn, and build the future. I enjoy visiting these spaces and seeing them filled with people and possibilities. I contribute to wealth and wellness in the communities I belong to, and I feel connected to the entrepreneurs who raised and taught me. It gives me a sense of Service that connects to my spirituality. My work is a tribute to them and my ancestors, which makes me feel that I have made them proud, and I am a living return on their investment. My style is also part of my expression. I always feel well dressed, confident, with effortless style. My home is comfortable and beautiful. Great views surround my home, and it is filled with memorable and meaningful pieces that remind me of family, friends, and a life well lived. My home is filled with love. It is a place for celebration and moments that will live in our hearts forever. We welcome all types of people with love and grace. I also have properties in our favorite places worldwide. Each space provides the perfect vibe for various parts of the year.

I am healthy—physically, mentally, and spiritually. I have a wonderful team of people, including a therapist, coach, and spiritual advisor, who I work with to keep me at peak health. I meditate, run, exercise, and stretch daily. I play basketball with friends and have activities such as golf and surfing that I have taken up. I have a nourishing diet that allows for a wide range of delicious foods I love. I feel good about myself. I am at a great weight, toned with a lean and muscular body. I take time each day for stillness and solitude. I am taking care of my body, mind, and spirit.

After a full day's activity, the evening ends with quality time with my wife and son. We talk about our days with reflection and gratitude. I have enough time for me to be quiet and check on those I love and hear about their lives. I have tended to myself and others to my satisfaction. I feel accomplished and serene as I know I did enough in alignment with my intentions and made a positive difference today. I ask for deep rest that will enlighten and recharge me for the next day ahead.

"**THE** MASTER IN THE ART OF LIVING MAKES LITTLE DISTINCTION BETWEEN HIS WORK AND HIS PLAY, HIS LABOR AND HIS LEISURE, HIS MIND AND HIS BODY, HIS INFORMATION AND HIS RECREATION, HIS LOVE AND HIS RELIGION. HE HARDLY KNOWS WHICH IS WHICH. HE SIMPLY PURSUES HIS VISION OF EXCELLENCE AT WHATEVER HE DOES, LEAVING OTHERS TO DECIDE WHETHER HE IS WORKING OR PLAYING. TO HIM HE'S ALWAYS DOING **BOTH.**"

—James A. Michener, American author

Afdhel's Living Vision

I wake up early in the morning in my house, before the sun has come up. My wife and son are asleep, so I savor this moment to be in service to my creativity.

I begin my day with meditation: I meditate every morning, giving me clarity, consciousness, calmness, and discernment.

I perform my three daily rituals: self-forgiveness (toward myself), self-acknowledgement (gratitude toward myself), and gratitude (toward others).

I have peace in my heart and help create that peace for others. There is no conflict in my life, just empathy with boundaries. I extend grace and forgiveness, knowing that I no longer need to be consumed by unnecessary conflict.

I have made peace with my ego and thank it for doing its job in protecting me. When conflict arises, I use my process of compassion, curiosity, creativity, and commitment to deal with it easily and quickly.

I am aware of how past traumas can create future conflict, and I am observant and patient with myself as I heal myself.

I am self-aware of upper limit problems that my ego may create to stop the continuous elevation of soul that is happening.

I have daily balance in the six dimensions of my life: health, family, work/wealth, creativity, relationships/community, and spirit/soul.

I make myself a coffee and sit down with my laptop and open up my brain to see what comes out. My mind is clear, and my thoughts flow from my soul to my fingertips, sometimes so fast that I can't keep up.

Ideas pour out of me, stories, concepts, insights, inspiration. Every day it is different, and every day it feels as if I am tapping into my Buddha brain, not my monkey brain.

I am an artist with the universe working through me.

My canvas is the world. The art that I am creating is a better future for our children and their children. I take pride in being a good ancestor.

The paints I choose to use vary: business, culture, art, story—but the subject is the same.

The story I am working on that fills me with hope is a new narrative for the world; one where everyone is living a joyful life of deep Purpose, in service to others and the planet.

This in turn creates the world we want to see: one where we have not only fixed the problems of our time but also have created a world that is blossoming and flourishing.

By the time I finish my work, my son is awake and I go and say hello and make him breakfast. I sit with him as we eat breakfast together, playing and doing a story—his favorite pastime, the thing that fills him up with love and attention and joy.

I am grateful for this time I have with him, just him and me. My job is to make sure he goes to school with a smile on his face.

After he and my wife leave for school, I go and exercise, feeling my heart race and my limbs stretch in preparation for the day.

I treat my body with the love and care that it deserves for being my incredible vehicle to journey through this life, for a long and fruitful time.

I realize that I can *create* time: by investing in my health, both physical and mental, I can extend my life to live longer and access even higher levels of joy.

I am here for a long time *and* a good time.

I feel a flood of energy, and my body feels good, ready for what is ahead.

I have a shower, and in my shorts, I walk barefoot in the grass to my studio, a place for creativity, joy, and inspiration.

My work is a series of conversations, which fuel my curiosity, feed my intelligence, and bring me constant wonder at the goodness of humanity. I speak to people around the world about the work they are doing and am constantly learning and expanding my mind about what is possible.

I am moved to tears by one project I am working on, the story of an ordinary person choosing to do an extraordinary thing—and seeing their community rise up to help them.

I am in awe at the goodness of people, the kindness of strangers, the possibilities for the human race to constantly exceed our limitations.

I enjoy being curious: I am a student as much as a teacher, because I believe the best teachers are always students. I love it when my learning curve is vertical.

I take delight in being out of my comfort zone, and I am constantly learning new creative media—music, film, experiences—because I believe they will make me a better storyteller. I am brave enough to suck at something new until I get better at it. The process and experience of learning is the reward, not the outcome.

I act out of a sense of devotion, not duty. My devotion is to my craft of being an artist and my Purpose—to inspire Purpose in the world, by bringing it alive.

I take a break to have lunch with my wife; we sit in the garden and eat a light meal, enjoying the sensation of sunshine on our bare legs, the butterflies and hummingbirds swooping above our heads. We talk about our day, how it's going, and we enjoy the easy intimacy of being with each other, in the home we have created together. We experience a thrill of anticipation as we talk about our next trip, visiting a new country and exploring its culture, its food, meeting its people—travel is one of our shared hobbies.

The rest of the afternoon, I am working again, more conversations about a rich diversity of creative projects where I am constantly growing as I expand beyond my understanding to learn something new and challenge myself. I feel secure in my knowledge that I have planned as best as I could for my family's financial stability, enough to give them a good life should anything happen to me.

My home is one of those places: a beautiful blend of nature and culture, family and work, friends and community. People who visit it come away feeling refreshed, relaxed, and restored in their spirit.

I create from a place of unconditional joy. I create in places that are beautiful and inspiring to me on an artistic and spiritual level. I leave space for constant connection to wonder and awe, through the power of nature.

I am an artist entrepreneur, making things that the world needs and desires and finding ways to turn that into abundance for myself and my family.

I live a life of grace and ease. I design my life not toward making more money but toward making more freedom: freedom in time and space, freedom from constraints and infrastructure.

I work only in my zone of genius, and I am blessed to have people around me working in theirs to make my life possible.

I laugh every day and try to make people around me laugh too.

Every day I do something for my mind, something for my body, something for my soul.

I am a coach and a friend to people who have incredible potential in the world, helping them see the possibilities by helping them find their Purpose and create a joyful life unique to them.

I am constantly inspired by collaborating with the best storytellers and artists in the world to help unleash their moral imaginations in Service of this new narrative.

I spark their imagination through the principles of this new story: joy, impact, courage, compassion, fun, coolness, and Service.

I am audaciously optimistic about the future of the world that I am helping create.

I ask questions instead of trying to provide answers.

I am open and receptive to what the universe sends my way.

I don't indulge in acts of self-sabotage: the only thing that can wreck this trajectory is me.

I say yes to less, to create room for the universe to cocreate with me, and I am constantly amazed by how much better the results are.

My faith is humanity: every day I have conversations with human beings who have chosen to do extraordinary things to make the world better, and it fills up my soul.

My religion is love: love for everyone around me, in a way that causes a ripple effect of love to flow outward from me in a silent, invisible conspiracy.

My daily practice is kindness: kindness to myself; through self-forgiveness and self-acknowledgement, I extend daily grace to myself.

By practicing kindness toward the people in my life I show them gratitude for the Gifts they give me every day.

I am a bringer of light into rooms.

I am in touch with my Sri Lankan culture, and I am deeply blessed to help the country thrive while also helping my son nurture a relationship with it.

Our son, now back from school, runs out to join us and demands a group hug; the two of us sandwiching him right between us fills me with a sense of gratitude and love that we get to spend so much time together in a peaceful, easy way.

In the afternoon, I finish work early and go for a bike ride with my son around our neighborhood, enjoying the sunshine on our faces as we pedal around. When we return, it's our turn to cook dinner, so we grill some healthy food on our barbecue, and my son proudly serves it to his mother, who claps her hands in appreciation. We snuggle into a couch for family movie night, a regular ritual where we laugh and are moved together by stories of fun and imagination.

We put our son to bed, and my wife and I have a glass of wine as we unwind and catch up about our days. My eyes light up as I tell her what brought me joy and inspiration. Finally, it is time to go to bed. I am happy because my day has been the perfect mix of family, creativity, work, exercise, and living, all integrated seamlessly. I have learned something new, I have been moved on a deeply emotional level, and I have tried to help as many people as I can. I have lived my day according to my own personal mantra:

> Time is more important than money. Experiences are more important than things. And therefore, time spent on experiences doing things you love, with the people you love, is the most important of all.
>
> I am in awe of the abundance around me, this life made possible through Purpose.
>
> The truth that has set me free is the realization that when you want something that is right for you, all the universe conspires with love in helping you to achieve it.

MY LIVING VISION

Now, it's your turn. Use these pages to start drafting your Living Vision.

CHAPTER 10

GIFTS

> The meaning of life is to find your Gift. The Purpose of life is
> to give it away.
>
> —Pablo Picasso, Spanish painter and sculptor

WHAT OUR GIFTS ARE

Our Gifts—those unique talents, skills, and abilities we each possess—
set each of us apart, allowing us to make our marks on the world around
us. These intrinsic "superpowers" are often celebrated and acknowledged
by our peers and colleagues, serving as the foundational essence of our
identity and influence. On our best days at work, we bring these special Gifts to the forefront, effortlessly navigating through challenges,
fostering innovation to solve problems, and inspiring others along the
way. Whether it's our leadership acumen, creative spark, or empathetic
approach, these Gifts are our personal treasures and our contributions to
the world around us. Within these Gifts are clues to endless possibilities
in our work and life.

   This case study is an example of how one person discovered a Gift
in a life-changing moment.

Case Study: Lindsey Roy – The Gift of Perspective

Lindsey Roy was living the dream. At age 31, she was named vice
president at Hallmark Cards—one of the youngest in the company's 100-plus-year history.

   But in a blink, her life was irrevocably changed. A boating
accident not only severed her left leg but left her with extensive
injuries to her right leg and arm. But amid the tragedy, Lindsey
found an unforeseen Gift—the Gift of perspective.

   With each day that brought feelings of loss and gratitude,
Lindsey began to see life through a lens colored with deeper

empathy, resilience, and an indomitable spirit to infuse goodness into the world. It was as though the universe had granted her a pair of what she calls "life goggles," reshaping her vision and, subsequently, her work and Purpose on Earth.

"Going through a life-altering accident certainly gave me a little bit more clarity about my Purpose here on Earth. My stated Purpose is to put good in the world, and I do through my role at Hallmark, but also as I try to raise my children to be empathetic and open-minded, and as a leader as I try to build people up, help them tap into their skills and value. I also try to put good in the world by being involved in my community and serving on boards that help people who have gone through things similar to me."

During the aftermath of the accident, as Lindsey navigated through the intricate dance of healing and rediscovering herself, Hallmark Cards' intrinsic Purpose—to help people care for one another—resonated with her newfound clarity. The company had long stood as a shining example of helping people express love and care for one another, providing just the words we yearn for to navigate the highs and lows of life.

In the midst of her recovery, Lindsey began to see the opportunities to use her Gifts to be of service through her work. As she shared her Gifts with us, she spoke about how she harnessed her natural abilities as a "connector" to bridge the gap between personal tragedy and professional Purpose. "I love to bring people together in all the ways," she reflected. Her knack for creating connections within the workplace and beyond translated into fostering a community spirit within Hallmark. Lindsey's high "empathy and emotional IQ" enabled her to infuse genuine understanding and compassion into her work, turning her ability to "read the room" into creating cards that could touch hearts

(continued)

(continued)

and offer solace. As an "idealist, dreamer, optimist," Lindsey's belief that "things will work out" influenced the hopeful essence of Hallmark's messaging. And as an "acceptor," her inclusive approach ensured that Hallmark's products were as diverse and wide-ranging as humanity itself, embracing all ways of expression without judgment or reservation.

But it was her Gift of perspective that inspired an innovation that touched the lives of millions. Lindsey realized that life is too short to celebrate only the significant milestones. Connecting this Gift with Hallmark's Purpose and an insight that, especially with all the divisive, challenging things around us, people are craving positive and good things, they created a line called "Just Because" cards. Designed to embody the spirit of "any day caring," these cards became notes of unwavering support and boundless love, not reserved just for grand occasions but available for the small, everyday moments that truly define life. Whether offering encouraging words to someone caught in the merciless clutches of cancer or giving praise to a child for a simple, kind act, the "Just Because" line serves as a companion through both joyous and challenging times alike.

"The idea for this line was partially informed by personal tragedy and the firm belief that we, as humans, are each experiencing our own tragedies and triumphs, and we could all use a little more care and love," Lindsey explained, her voice steady and sure.

Lindsey and her team at Hallmark drew deeply from the pain and lessons learned from personal experiences. They saw this line as an opportunity to bring hope and light when many need it most. Each card became a little love note, sometimes providing quiet comfort, at other times louder affirmations, but all providing a moment of joy.

The public embraced "Just Because" with open arms, finding in its delicate paper folds a friend, a confidante, and an ally bearing witness to their life journeys. The line sparked millions of moments of kindness and care.

Lindsey has begun sharing her story beyond the corridors of Hallmark as a speaker and author of her first book, *The Gift of Perspective*.

"In my talk, I say I'm here to offer these lessons for free. You don't have to get run over by a boat and dance with a propeller. Trust me, this is a better option!"

Lindsey offers an essential reminder that Purpose is a journey, not a destination.

Eight years after her accident, Lindsey, now fully adapted and thriving, faced a new trial: she was diagnosed with a rare and progressive disease that destroyed the blood vessels in her lungs, requiring a double-lung transplant. This setback urged a shift in perspective, prompting Lindsey to seek hidden advantages and unearth deeper resilience within herself.

"I still have quiet, prayerful moments and moments of reflection in which I continue to check in with myself, asking, 'Am I doing enough? Am I doing what I'm supposed to be doing?' I feel like I'm absolutely walking down that road, but I'm still on the journey."

EXERCISE: UNDERSTANDING YOUR GIFTS

Let's get started! Here are some questions for you to think about and complete.

1. Make a list of what you believe your top five Gifts are. In what areas do you believe you are strongest?

2. Ask your Purpose Posse the same question—what are your top five Gifts from their perspective? How have your Gifts made a positive impact in their lives?

3. In the circles on an upcoming page, write down the top three words that appear in both lists—yours and the ones that your Purpose Posse told you. The ones that appear the most are the ones that you should make a note of for the next stage.

Here is a list of some Gifts to get you started:

- Empathy
- Creativity
- Leadership

- Planning
- Innovation
- Communication
- Resilience
- Vision
- Dexterity
- Mentorship
- Curiosity
- Endurance
- Problem-solving
- Programming
- Adaptability

EXERCISE: WHAT ARE MY GIFTS?

1. _____
   _____

2. _____
   _____

3. _____
   _____

4. _____
   _____

5. _____
   _____

MY GIFTS

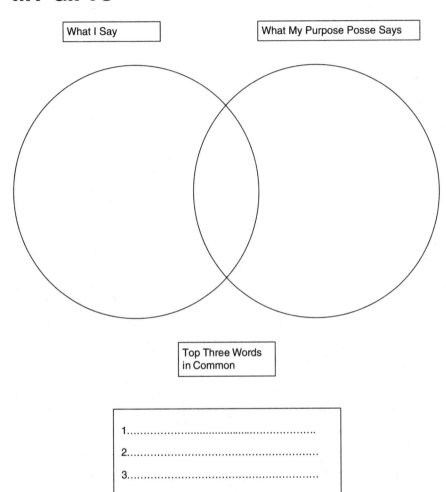

What I Say

What My Purpose Posse Says

Top Three Words
in Common

1...
2...
3...

CHAPTER 11
PASSIONS

> Working hard for something we don't care about is called stress.
> Working hard for something we love is called Passion.
> —Simon Sinek, English American author and inspirational speaker

WHAT OUR PASSIONS ARE

Our Passions are the driving forces that make us come alive, propelling us with energy toward causes, ideas, or endeavors that deeply resonate with our core. These are the sparks that ignite our spirits, getting us to leap out of bed each morning with a zest for life and a desire to contribute. They are connected to the issues that stir our souls, the ideas that spark our imagination, and the causes that speak to our hearts, compelling us to engage, to act, and to advocate. Whether it's a commitment to social justice, a love for the environment, or a dedication to a creative pursuit, our Passions are the fire that light up our paths, infusing each day with meaning and directing our steps toward making a difference in the areas that matter most to us.

This case study is about an intrapreneur whose Passion for social justice came alive following the tragic murder of one of his relatives.

Case Study: Aaron Mitchell – Helping Netflix Invest in Solving the Racial Wealth Gap

The bright lights of Netflix illuminated millions of screens, providing solace and distraction for many during the tumultuous days of 2020. But behind the screens, in the halls of the corporate giant, an equally compelling story was unfolding. And the protagonist of this story wasn't a Hollywood star. It was an HR executive named Aaron Mitchell, who was ready to act.

The year commenced with heartbreak for Aaron, as his cousin was murdered by police in a tragic shooting in January. The ensuing chaos wrought by the COVID-19 pandemic left little room for personal grief, as Aaron juggled the demands of family life and the new realities of a world in crisis. And then came another crucible moment for Aaron—the tragic murder of George Floyd, an act that shook the world to its core.

In an effort to reconnect amid these challenging times, Aaron convened a dinner with friends and colleagues. It was during this gathering that a conversation on bridging the racial and economic chasms in marginalized communities took a decisive turn, sparking Aaron's interest in the potential of redirecting corporate funds to Black banks, which aligned with his Passions for bringing people together.

"My goal has always been to help people build bridges so that we can all participate in the evolution of our humanity."

Driven by this Passion and a newfound curiosity, Aaron delved into the structural intricacies of Black banking through Mehrsa Baradaran's *The Color of Money*, gaining insights into the racial wealth gap's systemic foundations. However, it was a Netflix original, *The Black Godfather*, that truly galvanized him into action.

"Watching *The Black Godfather* and Clarence Avant's example: Being in the room and making stuff happen when the cameras weren't rolling. I didn't want to be in the room and in the proximity of such power without doing the same. That and we needed to do something to address systemic racism in a way that mattered."

Moved by Clarence Avant's behind-the-scenes influence, Aaron resolved to convene colleagues to channel Netflix's considerable clout toward effecting meaningful change against systemic racism. Aaron brought forth a proposal to earmark a segment of Netflix's cash holdings for Black banking institutions, aiming to catalyze a significant shift in capital.

Despite initial ambivalence by some, Spencer Neumann, Netflix's CFO, recognized the potential of Aaron's vision, encouraging further

(continued)

(continued)

exploration and using *The Black Godfather* as an inspiration to finalize the proposal. Neumann's support was crucial in navigating internal skepticism.

The urgency of Aaron's mission was magnified by his cousin's death, a pain that had lingered unaddressed until George Floyd's murder by a Minneapolis police officer. This event not only reignited Aaron's unresolved grief but also underscored the critical need for immediate response that could turn corporate concern and allyship for the Black community in America into meaningful and sustainable action.

Netflix's groundbreaking pledge in June 2020 to redirect 2% of its cash reserves—initially amounting to $100 million—into Black financial institutions marked a historic moment. Aaron recognized the indispensable role of allies in this journey, lauding the monumental collective effort that brought this initiative to fruition.

"I could write an entire article about the cast of very important people that made this initiative possible," he said, underlining the communal effort.

His Passion for this work was magnified when he saw the impact on financial institutions such as HOPE Credit Union, which serves members throughout Alabama, Arkansas, Louisiana, Mississippi, and Tennessee, shaping policies and practices that have improved conditions in opportunity deserts nationwide. Through the 2% pledge, HOPE underwent significant transformation, leveraging Netflix's commitment to rally further support and unlock tremendous capital, buoying other corporations' trust in Black institutions.

The journey, however, was not just about capital movement. It was about consciously integrating values, fostering trust and partnership, and intentionally curating relationships. Mitchell's advice to other corporate leaders? "Keep it simple."

The initiative's scope extended beyond mere financial investment, incorporating a component of knowledge sharing as well. Prompted by Mehrsa Baradaran and with Reed Hastings's endorsement—who remarked, "It's so capitalistic it warms my heart"—Aaron developed a playbook to guide other corporations in joining the movement. This effort, in collaboration with Shannon Alwyn, Netflix's treasurer, highlighted the initiative's community-focused ethos.

"It's about a collective endeavor, deeply rooted in my Passion. Engagement must be a team effort," Aaron stressed.

Aaron's work continues, and his invitation for others to join remains open. "To help close the wealth gap, we need more companies to join this movement. If your company is interested in how it works, you can check out what we've learned at aaronmitchell .com. Together, we can contribute to more healing and progress for Black communities."

"SUCCESS ISN'T ABOUT WHAT YOU MAKE, IT'S ABOUT THE DIFFERENCE YOU MAKE IN PEOPLE'S LIVES."

—Michelle Obama, former First Lady of the United States

UNDERSTANDING YOUR PASSIONS

We're about to ask you to do the same exercise you did with Gifts. But first is a list of questions for you to consider as you think about your Passions:

1. **Your Passions versus your hobbies:** Your Passions aren't the same as your hobbies, such as music or cooking. These are about what social and environmental or issues you get passionate about wanting to solve. What gets you mad? What breaks your heart? What makes you get out of bed in the morning? What are you most passionate about? Take a look at the next page if you need help distinguishing between your Passions and hobbies.

2. **Look at your own history:** Perhaps there is something about your story that represents a challenge you had to overcome. Maybe you are a member of a marginalized group or come from a lower income background. Maybe you have family members who have been affected by adversity. Maybe you were a victim of violence. Understanding your own story may help you unearth clues as to what you are drawn to helping others overcome. It may have happened to you, but perhaps part of your Purpose is helping to avoid it happening to others.

3. **Volunteering:** Do you volunteer or donate to any nonprofits outside of work? Perhaps it's a cause that is close to your heart, such as hunger in families, or something related to your local community. Identifying issues that you are already donating your time and money to is a great first step.

4. **Look at what your company focuses on solving:** Perhaps there is a list of nonprofits or causes that your company is already involved in. Look through the internal communications to see if there is something that immediately tugs at your heart.

5. **Look at the United Nations Sustainable Development Goals:** If you're stuck for inspiration, consider checking out the UN SDGs: these are a list of the world's biggest problems, from education to gender equality. Read through some of the projects online to see if any inspire you.

The Difference between Passion and a Hobby

Passion	Hobby
Definition: An interest or goal that you invest time and effort into to grow in your personal or professional life	Definition: An activity done regularly in your leisure time for pleasure
Something you do because you can't stop thinking about it	Something that occupies your mind only when you are doing it
Time: You find time to do it	Time: You only do it in your free time
Motivation: Meaning	Motivation: Fun
Example: Creating a beach clean-up club	Example: Going to the beach

EXERCISE: WHAT ARE MY PASSIONS?

Let's get started! Here is a list of questions for you to think about and complete.

1. Make a list of what you believe your top five Passions are.

2. Ask your Purpose Posse the same question—what do they think are your top five Passions?

3. In the circles on the next page, write down the top three words that appear in both lists—yours and the ones that your Purpose Posse told you. The ones that appear the most are the ones that you should make note of.

Here are some ideas for Passions to get your juices flowing:

- Mental health
- Racial justice
- Healing and growth
- Gender equality
- Protecting the planet
- Helping veterans
- Helping your local community
- Hunger and malnutrition
- Homelessness
- Education
- Protecting animals
- Raising consciousness

1. _____

   _____

2. _____

   _____

3. _____

   _____

4. _____

   _____

5. _____

   _____

MY PASSIONS

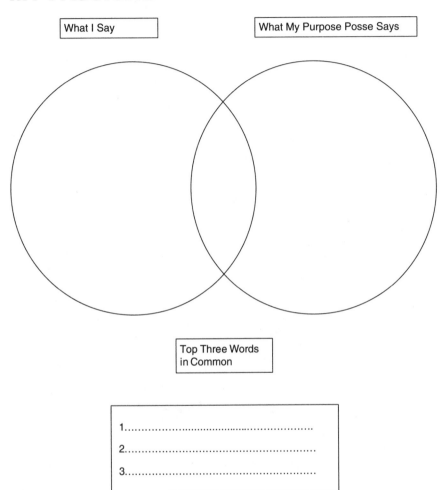

What I Say

What My Purpose Posse Says

Top Three Words in Common

1...
2...
3...

CHAPTER 12

SERVICE

Service to others is the rent you pay for your room
here on Earth.

—Muhammad Ali, American professional boxer and activist

SERVICE DEFINED

Every individual possesses a unique combination of Gifts and Passions that define their essence and trajectory. These are the factors that not only differentiate us from one another but also empower us to create significant value for our organizations and the wider world.

Our innate Gifts, those special talents and skills, act as our "superpowers," paving the way for remarkable accomplishments and catalyzing innovation. On the other hand, our Passions provide the fuel that drives us, pushing us toward endeavors that resonate with our souls and compelling us to champion causes that truly matter.

When used in Service, our Gifts and Passions create a powerful synergy, enabling us to transcend the ordinary, inspire those around us, and make a profound impact.

As you embark on the next step of your journey, you'll delve deep into how your Gifts and Passions can serve not just your company but also your community and beyond.

The following inspiring case study is of an intrapreneur who went on a journey of innovation and inclusivity that resulted in a billion-dollar movie—and the reinvention of an American icon.

Case Study: Kim Culmone – Reinventing Barbie at Mattel

Kim Culmone's remarkable journey to the head of Design of Dolls at Mattel is a testament to the power of aligning one's Gifts and Passions with Service that creates career success and ripple effects of impact that have reshaped our world. It's a story of transformation, not just for an iconic brand but for countless people worldwide touched by her vision and dedication.

We spoke with Kim about her journey, starting with her Gifts. She talked about her unique strengths with a touch of vulnerability, saying, "I find that the Gift thing makes me feel self-conscious at first." But she shares that "I'm a really curious person" and that relentless desire to understand the why behind every decision propels her leadership at Mattel. This curiosity isn't just about products or strategies; it's a genuine interest in people, a cornerstone of her approach to leadership. "I care about the people I lead," she shares, underlining the Gifts of warmth and authenticity she brings to her role.

Kim also spoke about her "bravery in communication," a quality that allows her to dive into tough discussions and articulate thoughts that others may shy away from. This bravery is not about confrontation but about creating a space where truth can surface, making it easier to navigate challenges and foster a collaborative environment. "I'm absolutely willing to have difficult conversations directly," she explains, emphasizing how this approach clears the air and promotes a culture of openness and respect.

These innate Gifts were evident at a young age, as was the beginnings of a lasting Passion for social justice.

Growing up in New Orleans, Kim was surrounded by the stark realities of racism, both within her family and the broader community. Despite her efforts to fight against it, many relatives harbored deeply racist views, often without recognizing them. Kim recalls a pivotal childhood moment that shaped her understanding of race and injustice. "I had been told not to play with Black kids," she shares, recounting how she unknowingly befriended a

(continued)

(continued)

Black girl at a public pool in Audubon Park. The joyous day they spent together was abruptly interrupted when she was pulled aside and scolded for interacting with the girl. This incident left a profound impact on Kim, instilling a deep sense of wrongness about the prejudices she was being taught. "I just remember in my tiny body, knowing how wrong that was," she reflects, marking the beginning of her lifelong commitment to challenging racial injustices. This early experience, coupled with her journey into her queer identity and a feminist upbringing, fueled her political involvement and advocacy for marginalized communities.

Her Passion for social justice is both personal and professional, guiding her efforts to create a more inclusive and fairer world. "It's just frustrating to me when less powerful groups in our society are abandoned or then politicized," she reflects, acknowledging the broader societal issues that fuel her work. Kim's leadership is not just about navigating a brand through the market's currents; it's a mission to uplift and empower, to ensure that every child can see themselves in the toys they play with and feels free to play with whomever they choose.

"In my view, my job encompasses not only the work I do and the things I create but also the people I lead and how I'm developing the next generation of leaders at my level," Kim shares, highlighting her commitment to Service. It's a perspective that views leadership not as a position of power but as a platform for impact. She understands the ripple effect of her role, aiming to inspire and shape future leaders who can carry forward the values of innovation, inclusivity, and social justice.

Kim's Purpose is crystallized in her dedicated area of Service: creating space for marginalized voices. "In my work, my Purpose is to create space for marginalized voices, whether that's in a meeting room, with a product, or in any other capacity, to utilize my platform to elevate those who are often unseen and unheard," she explains. This commitment is not just rhetoric; it's reflected in the diversity of the dolls under her leadership, such as American Girl and Monster High, to the groundbreaking success of Barbie. Kim uses her platform to elevate those often unseen and unheard, ensuring they're not just included but celebrated.

Under Kim's stewardship, Barbie has undergone a radical transformation. Once criticized for promoting a narrow standard of beauty, the brand now champions diversity, inclusivity, and empowerment. Kim's vision has turned Barbie into a mirror reflecting the world's rich eclecticism, allowing children to find themselves in their playthings. This shift is not merely cosmetic; it's a cultural statement, asserting the importance of representation and the value of every individual's story.

It returned the doll to being a billion-dollar brand after years spent languishing. But it also had an immense impact on young girls who finally saw themselves recognized in the rainbow diversity of the new Barbie. Without that groundwork laid by Kim, the filmmakers Greta Gerwig and Margot Robbie would not have had the starting point to craft their powerful *Barbie* movie that so deftly wove in themes of empowerment and liberation and went on to inspire even more people (not to mention a billion-dollar box office return).

Kim's journey with Barbie, marked by her innate Gifts, deep Passions, and dedicated Service, embodies a powerful narrative of change. It's a story of how one person's commitment to their values can redefine an iconic brand and, in doing so, inspire a new generation to embrace their unique identities. Kim's work with Barbie is more than a career highlight; it's a legacy of empowerment, a testament to the impact of leading with Purpose, authenticity, and an unwavering belief in the potential of every child to shape a more inclusive and compassionate world.

EXERCISE: HOW CAN I BE OF SERVICE?

Let's get started! The following list of questions are for you to think about and complete.

1. Make a list of what you believe your top five areas of Service are, and keep in mind that some people (as in Kim's example) are more drawn to being of Service to individuals, whereas others may be more drawn to be of Service to their organizations (such as Lindsey) or their communities (such as Aaron). There is no right or wrong answer; it's just where you intuitively feel drawn to. Here are some ideas for Service to get your juices flowing:

- Your family and friends
- Your fellow employees
- Your local community
- Your city
- Your country
- The planet
- Underserved groups: women and girls
- Underserved groups: marginalized communities
- Underserved groups: at-risk youth
- Underserved groups: people of color
- An idea or cause that you are determined to support

2. Explore whether there is a natural link from your Gifts and Passions.

For example, if your Passions are helping women and girls, and your Gifts are communication and storytelling, there may be a girls education nonprofit locally who needs help in getting their message across that you can offer your services to.

3. Ask your Purpose Posse the same—what do they think are your top five areas where your Gifts and Passions can be of Service?

How have they seen you be of service to them in the past? This is a great opportunity to better understand the impact you are already having in the world.

4. In the circles on the next page, write down the top three words that appear in both lists—yours and the ones that your Purpose Posse told you. The ones that appear the most are the ones that you should make a note of for the next stage.

Individuals (e.g., family, friends)

_____

_____

Teams (e.g., team at work)

_____

_____

Company

_____

_____

Community (e.g., a specific community you belong to)

_____

_____

Cause (e.g., a cause you feel passionate about)

_____

_____

City (e.g., your neighborhood or town)

_____

_____

Country

_____

_____

Society/the World

_____

_____

MY AREAS OF SERVICE

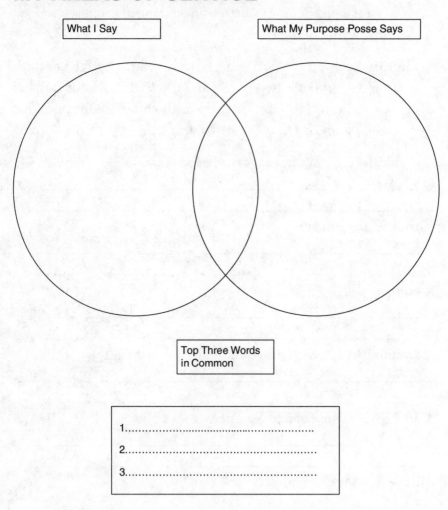

What I Say

What My Purpose Posse Says

Top Three Words
in Common

1...

2...

3...

CHAPTER 13

PUTTING IT ALL TOGETHER: YOUR PERSONAL PURPOSE STATEMENT

> The two most important days in your life are the day you are
> born and the day you find out why.
> —**Mark Twain, American author and humorist**

Now *it's time to put everything together!* Take a moment to look back at your Gifts, Passions, and Service pages and pick the top three from each list—the ones that both you and your Purpose Posse identified, that showed up in the middle of each Venn diagram. Now you can begin to put them together in the form of a sentence.

My Purpose is to use my Gifts of:

1. _____
_____

2. _____
_____

3. _____
_____

And my Passions of:

1. _____
_____

2. _____
_____

3. _____
_____

To be of Service to:

1. _____
_____

2. _____

   _____

3. _____

   _____

Take a moment to read your Purpose statement out loud. How does that sound? Does it resonate with you? If the answer is not yet, consider revisiting your Gifts and Passions to refine your statement until it feels genuinely aligned with who you are.

GOING FURTHER: WRITING A TWO-WORD PURPOSE STATEMENT

This section is a bit more advanced! Feel free to skip it and come back to it later.

We find it is powerful to try and condense a Purpose statement down to two words. That's right, two words (okay, maybe three, max!). A verb and a noun.

Let's take a look at some examples from Afdhel and Bobby's journey. Bobby's longer GPS statement was:

> *To use my Gifts of moral imagination and creating connectedness and my Passion for entrepreneurship and mentorship to be of service by feeding the good in myself, the communities I belong to, and the world I share with others.*

From there, he was able to distil it down into three words: *Feeding the Good*.

Afdhel's longer GPS statement was:

> *To use my Gifts of storytelling against my Passion of inspiring Purpose to be of Service to people and organizations.*

From there, he was able to distil it down into two words: *Inspiring Purpose*.

When you look at your longer GPS statement, see if there is one particular verb and one particular noun that really stand out in terms of power and energy. Try taking them out of the longer statement and writing them down as a two-word phrase.

Here are some two-word Purpose statements that we love:

- Building Bridges
- Healing Wounds
- Connecting People
- Spreading Joy
- Discovering Truth
- Finding Connection
- Telling Stories

EXERCISE: MY TWO-WORD PURPOSE STATEMENT

Take some time and write down some possible combinations here.

GETTING IN ALIGNMENT WITH YOUR ASSIGNMENT

Now comes the good stuff! How can you align your personal Purpose with your organization's Purpose?

A caveat: this assumes that your place of work gives you a feeling of psychological safety and belonging, that you feel like you are paid well with commensurate benefits.

These are prerequisites to being able to find Purpose in your work. If someone is feeling scared in a toxic workplace, it is impossible for them to be in a mental state to be able to seek Purpose.

Remember Maslow's hierarchy of needs? Purpose can only be achieved when all your other needs are met.

No job is perfect; there are always going to be things that you wish were better. But finding your Purpose and aligning it to your role inside the organization is one sure-fire way to head in the right direction.

"PEOPLE MAY SPEND THEIR WHOLE LIVES CLIMBING THE LADDER OF SUCCESS ONLY TO FIND, ONCE THEY REACH THE TOP, THAT THE LADDER IS LEANING AGAINST THE WRONG WALL."

—Thomas Merton

EXERCISE: APPLYING PURPOSE TO MY WORK

These questions will help you think about how to apply all the Purpose principles discussed so far to your work, and specifically to your career/ profession. Think through these questions and consider what role you believe Purpose can and should play.

Start by placing your company or organization's Purpose statement (if it has one) next to your own. Do you see an immediate overlap between what it stands for and what your Purpose is?

The stronger the overlap, the deeper the connection you will have to your organization, and the more meaning you will be able to find in your work.

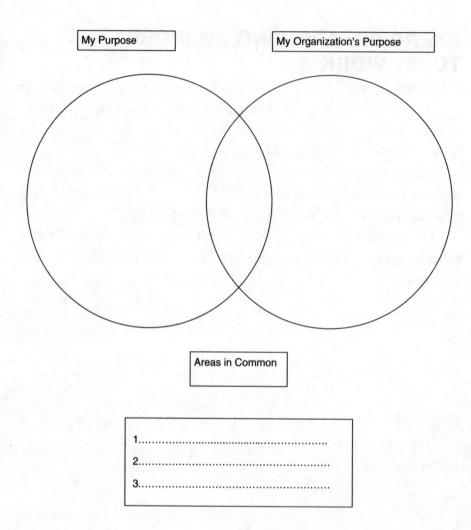

My Purpose

My Organization's Purpose

Areas in Common

1..

2..

3..

If the answer isn't immediately apparent, take some time to think through the following questions.

1. **How can you better understand your company's Purpose?** Consider how you can dig deeper to truly understand the company's mission and values. Engage with leadership or seek out the department responsible for crafting the Purpose statement to learn about the story and ideas behind it.

   Action step: Schedule a meeting with a member of the leadership team (for example, a chief marketing officer, chief impact officer, or chief sustainability officer) or the department that created the Purpose statement. Prepare questions to learn about the history, motivations, and aspirations behind the company's Purpose. This deeper understanding can enhance your connection to the company and inform how you contribute to its mission.

   _____

   _____

   _____

   _____

   _____

2. **What aspects of my job align with my personal values?** Reflect on the parts of your job that resonate most with your Purpose and values. Are there specific tasks, projects, or responsibilities that feel particularly meaningful or fulfilling?

   Action step: Join an Employee Resource Group (ERG) that brings you into contact with fellow employees who are passionate about things you are. This could be diversity, mental health, LGBTQ representation, AAPI representation, and so many more. Find allies—you don't have to do this alone.

_____

_____

_____

_____

_____

3. **How can I make a positive impact in my role?** Consider how your position in the company allows you to make a difference. What unique Gifts or perspectives do you bring to your role that can contribute positively to your team, the company, or even the wider community?

   Action step: Explore any volunteering and fundraising programs that exist in your company that align with your Passion. This is a great, lightweight way to start exploring that kinds of issues and causes that bring you alive.

_____

_____

_____

_____

_____

4. **What goals do you want to achieve in your career, and how do they align with your company's Purpose?** Think about your long-term career objectives and how they align with the mission and goals of the organization. How can your current role help you progress toward these personal and professional aspirations?

   Action step: Share your GPS statement with your manager, peers, and even your direct reports and talk to them about your long-term aspirations. Together, you may be able to plot a path to another internal role that brings you even more meaning. For instance, if it's sustainability you're interested in, there may be a role in your company's sustainability department that you can transition to.

_____

_____

_____

_____

_____

HOW CAN LEADERS CREATE A SENSE OF PURPOSE AT WORK?

Here are some ways for leaders to encourage a sense of Purpose in the workplace and help their teams get even more in alignment with their assignment:

- Start with "why": Always look at problems and opportunities through the first principles of Purpose.
- Make work matter: Show your employees how their work ladders up to a higher Purpose.
- Create opportunities for Purpose growth and learning: bring in speakers on Purpose and create Purpose book clubs.
- Support the intrapreneurs: ensure you pay your ERGs extra for the work they do as ambassadors of Purpose.
- Fireworks and bonfires: give rewards and recognition for Purpose in small moments (bonfires, for instance, in a weekly meeting) and in bigger moments (fireworks, for instance, an annual Day of Purpose).
- Regularly show people how their work benefits others: think of monthly Purpose awards celebrating people who live their Purpose, and create a surround sound of stories that fuels a Purpose-driven culture.

- Help people tie their everyday tasks to a bigger Purpose: always help them reframe their work from the mundane to the magnificent.
- Make contribution goals as important as achievement goals: make sure your incentive structure has Purpose goals built into it, both big and small.
- Foster a sense of Purpose outside of work: understand that your employees are people with rich lives outside of work.
- Coaching: Leverage your internal learning and development networks and bring in Purpose coaches

A Purpose-driven culture can improve employee motivation and productivity. Employees who have a strong sense of Purpose are more likely to give their best effort. They are also able to better cope when facing adversity.

IN CLOSING

> You can't go back and change the beginning, but you can start
> where you are and change the ending.
> —C.S. Lewis, British writer

You made it! Congratulations on making it through to the end.

We hope that reading this book and hearing about our own journey as two regular employees who went on a quest together to find their Purpose helps you realize that this a path open to anyone.

We also hope that you now have a better understanding of what personal Purpose is—and we hope that you are now clearer about your own Gifts, Passions, and how you can be of Service to others.

PURPOSE IS NOT JUST ABOUT GIVING BACK: IT'S ABOUT PAYING IT FORWARD

As we write these words, the world seems in a more tumultuous and toxic place than ever before. More hopeless than at any time in living memory.

But what gives us hope is you.

You and millions of others like you, who are embarking on a journey to not only find their Purpose but find ways to use the awesome power of business to unleash forces of good.

To do that, we need one thing: for you to come alive. That's why we wrote this book—about how you can find a meaningful and prosperous career by discovering your personal Purpose.

We see this book as the third in our *Purpose Trilogy*, completing the trifecta on how to lead with Purpose (*Good Is the New Cool Guide to Conscious Business: How Companies Can Drive Growth Through Positive Impact*), create with Purpose (*Good Is the New Cool Guide to Meaningful*

Marketing: How Brands Can Win with Conscious Consumers), and finally work with Purpose (this book you are holding).

Together they form a blueprint for how we can reimagine capitalism to be a force for responsible, inclusive growth—and good. And we think this couldn't come at a more significant time in human history. We are in a truly unique moment as a species.

We are wise enough to know how we are unwittingly causing our own destruction—through climate change, through war, through greed—but also through other potentially dangerous technologies such as artificial intelligence.

But we are not wise enough to know how to solve all these problems that we've created.

That is why we believe the answer is Purpose: helping individuals like you understand the enormous power you have within you to make positive change happen in the world, and then using your Purpose to give you courage, clarity, focus, and determination.

When we think about Purpose, we believe that it is not only about giving back to the teams, communities, and societies we are part of. It is also about paying it forward to the next generations—our children and our children's children.

In this moment, we need to be good ancestors - and have the moral maturity and clarity to understand how our actions (or inactions) will have a ripple effect for centuries to come. We need to be conscious about what we can do in the here and now, to understand that our courage and our sacrifice now will benefit people we may never meet.

There's a great Greek proverb: "A society grows great when old men plant trees in whose shade they never sit."

Let's plant some trees together.

—Afdhel and Bobby

References

Anderson, R. J., and Adams, W. A. 2015. *Mastering Leadership: An Integrated Framework for Breakthrough Performance and Extraordinary Business Results*. Hoboken, NJ: Wiley & Sons.

Benevity. 2018. "Benevity Study Links Employee-Centric Corporate Goodness Programs to Big Gains in Retention." https://benevity.com/press-releases/benevity-study-links-employee-centric-corporate-goodness-programs-big-gains.

BetterUp. 2018. "Workers Value Meaning at Work; New Research from BetterUp Shows Just How Much They're Willing to Pay for It." https://www.betterup.com/press/workers-value-meaning-at-work-new-research-from-betterup-shows-just-how-much-theyre-willing-to-pay-for-it.

Blount, S., and Leinwand, P. 2019. "Why Are We Here? If You Want Employees Who Are More Engaged and Productive, Give Them a Purpose—One Concretely Tied to Your Customers and Your Strategy." *Harvard Business Review* 2019 (November–December), pp. 1–9.

Boreham, I. D., and Schutte, N. S. 2023. "The Relationship between Purpose in Life and Depression and Anxiety: A Meta-analysis."

Journal of Clinical Psychology 79(12). https://doi.org/10.1002/jclp
.23576.

Feldman, J. n.d. "Purpose Powered Success." Korn Ferry. https://www
.kornferry.com/insights/this-week-in-leadership/purpose-powered-
success.

Gallup. 2019. https://www.gallup.com/workplace/247391/fixable-
problem-costs-businessestrillion.aspx.

Gallup. 2023. "State of the Global Workplace: 2023 Report." https://
www.gallup.com/workplace/349484/state-of-the-global-workplace-
2022-report.aspx.

Gartner. 2023. "Employees Seek Personal Value and Purpose at Work. Be
Prepared to Deliver." https://www.gartner.com/en/articles/employees-
seek-personal-value-and-purpose-at-work-be-prepared-to-deliver.

Garton, E., and Mankins, M. 2015. "Engaging Your Employees Is Good,
but Don't Stop There." Harvard Business Review, December 9, 2015.
https://hbr.org/2015/12/engaging-your-employees-is-good-but-
dont-stop-there.

Goleman, D. n.d. "Millenials: The Purpose Generation." Korn Ferry.
https://www.kornferry.com/insights/this-week-in-leadership/
millennials-purpose-generation.

Gurchiek, K. 2014. "'Millennial's Desire to Do Good Defines Workplace
Culture: Examine Community Service Programs to 'Seal the Deal.'"
Society for Human Resource Management, July 7, 2014. https://
www.shrm.org/topics-tools/news/inclusion-diversity/millennials-
desire-to-good-defines-workplace-culture.

Hendricks, G. 2010. *The Big Leap: Conquer Your Hidden Fear and Take Life to the Next Level.* New York: HarperCollins.

Hill, P. L., Turiano, N. A., Mroczek, D. K., and Burrow, A. L. 2016. "The Value of a Purposeful Life: Sense of Purpose Predicts Greater Income and Net Worth." *Journal of Research in Personality* 65, pp. 38–42. https://www.sciencedirect.com/science/article/abs/pii/S0092656616300836.

Hurst, A., Vestyesty, L., Pearce, A., Schnidman, A., Erickson, C., Garlinghouse, M., Parish, S., and Pavela, A. 2016. "2016 Workforce Purpose Index. Purpose at Work: The Largest Global Study on the Role of Purpose in the Workforce." Imperative. https://40823263.fs1.hubspotusercontent-na1.net/hubfs/40823263/Content%20Downloads/2016%20Workforce%20Purpose%20Index.pdf.

IBM Institute for Business Value. 2015. "Myths, Exaggerations and Uncomfortable Truths: The Real Story Behind Millennials in the Workplace."

Kim, E. S., Chen, Y., Nakamura, J. S., Ryff, C. D., and VanderWeele, T. J. 2022. "Sense of Purpose in Life and Subsequent Physical, Behavioral, and Psychosocial Health: An Outcome-Wide Approach." *American Journal of Health Promotion* 36(1), pp. 137–147. https://doi.org/10.1177/08901171211038545.

O'Brien, D., Main, A., Kounkel, S., and Stephan, A. R. 2019. "Purpose Is Everything." Deloitte Insights. https://www2.deloitte.com/us/en/insights/topics/marketing-and-sales-operations/global-marketing-trends/2020/purpose-driven-companies.html.

Schaefer, S. M., Morozink Boylan, J., Van Reekum, C. M., Lapate, R. C., Norris, C. J., Ryff, C. D., et al. 2013. "Purpose in Life Predicts Better

Emotional Recovery from Negative Stimuli." *PLoS ONE* 8(11), p. e80329. https://doi.org/10.1371/journal.pone.0080329.

Science of Purpose. n.d. http://scienceofpurpose.org/.

Thurman, H. 2010. *The Living Wisdom of Howard Thurman: A Visionary for Our Time*. Louisville, CO: Sounds True.

Urban Land Institute (ULI). 2014. "The Human Era @ Work: Findings from the Energy Project and Harvard Business Review." https://uli.org/wp-content/uploads/ULI-Documents/The-Human-Era-at-Work.pdf.

ABOUT
THE AUTHORS

Afdhel Aziz is one of the most inspiring leaders in the global movement of business as a force for good.

A former Fortune 500 business executive, he embarked on a remarkable journey after surviving the devastating tsunami in his home country of Sri Lanka. This life-altering experience prompted him to seek a deeper Purpose beyond the confines of corporate life.

In 2017, Afdhel made a pivotal decision to leave the corporate world and establish Conspiracy of Love as a B Corp certified global consultancy and proud minority-owned business.

He is now the cofounder and chief Purpose officer of Conspiracy of Love, a global purposeful growth consultancy with blue chip clients such as Adidas, Sephora, The Gap, and many more.

As an international keynote speaker, he has inspired audiences at leading corporations such as Disney, Microsoft, JPMorgan Chase, and The Gap, as well as prestigious venues such as the United Nations, the Cannes Lions, and the Fast Company Innovation Festival. He is also cofounder of Good is the New Cool, a creative studio focused on filling the hope gap with stories of inspiration, innovation, and impact. Good is the New Cool produces books, podcasts, TV shows, and a global conference series called GOODCon, which is hosted in Los Angeles, London, Sydney, Toronto, and New York.

Afdhel's prowess as an award-winning poet (*China Bay Blues*), novelist (*Strange Fruit*), and documentary film director (*The Genius of the Place*) underscores his fascination with the art and craft of storytelling.

On a personal note, he is a proud adoptive father, residing in Los Angeles with his wife, son, and an adorable beagle named Archie.

Find out more at www.afdhelaziz.com

Bobby Jones is a visionary entrepreneur and inspiring storyteller whose work has helped leaders in over 150 countries to drive meaningful growth and impact.

Bobby's highly demanded keynotes and workshops empower audiences with road maps to find lasting fulfillment and meaning in their work, sparking a fire that transforms their lives, work, and the world for the better.

Bobby is cofounder of Conspiracy of Love, which is accelerating the business success of the world's leading companies, including Adidas, Haleon, Unilever, Gap Inc., Mondelez, Diageo, and PepsiCo, profitably growing their brands, markets, people, and cultures by adding value to society.

He is also cofounder of Good is the New Cool, a creative studio focused on filling the *hope gap* with stories of inspiration, innovation, and impact. Good is the New Cool produces books, podcasts, TV shows, and a global conference series called GOODCon, which is hosted in Los Angeles, London, Sydney, Toronto, and New York.

Bobby's latest venture, RIVET, is a Gen Z–focused social enterprise that partners with popular brands to fund youth-led change through consumer purchases. By bringing together brands, influencers, and NGOs, RIVET will invest over $250 million in youth-led social innovation over the next decade.

With every venture, keynote address, and creative act, Bobby Jones fulfills his Purpose of feeding the good in himself, the communities he belongs to, and the world he shares with others.

Bobby lives in Brooklyn, New York, with his wife and son.

Learn more at www.bobbyjonesonpurpose.com

THANKS AND ACKNOWLEDGMENTS

Our journey to building a life of Purpose, Passion, and prosperity would have been all the longer and harder if it weren't for these companions along the way who made it easier.

Our Conspiracy of Love crew: Helen Trickey, Philipp Reker, Faye "Mouse" Bell, Veronika Monteith, Lucia Slezakowa, Katie Denman, Chloe Matharu, Alec Harden-Henry, Marissa Green, Manu Rios-Krauss, Catrin Thomas, Rena Varsani, Lucie Greene, Jean Batthany, Neil Dusuki, Ann Ohrling, Michele Lee, Tim O'Brien, Denise Roberson, Anuska Bharvani, Hoby Wedler, David Oswald, and all our Co-Conspirators around the world.

The courageous companies and brands who have trusted us along this journey: The a2 Milk Company, Adidas, Akamai, Alicorp, American Family Insurance, Athleta, Banana Republic, Bare, belVita, Benevity, Bimbo Bakeries USA, Bolivar, BUILD, Chips Ahoy!, The Coca-Cola Company, Cotton On Foundation, Crate and Barrel, Crown Royal, Diageo, GAP, Giant Spoon, GSK, Haleon, HALLS, Hewlett-Packard, Hotaling & Co., The Laundress, Inc., LG, Molson Coors, Mucinex, Natean, Nespresso, Negrita, Nexium, Nike, Off The Eaten Path, Old Navy, OREO, PepsiCo, Project Management Institute, Ritz, Robitussin, Sara Lee, Sephora, Skittles, Sour Patch Kids, Stacy's, Starry, Sun Life, Swedish Fish, The Laundress, Inc., Trident, and Unilever Australia.

Our courageous clients (the wider Conspiracy of Love) who are trying to make change everyday: Menake Gopinath, Pierre Le Manh, Lenka Pincot, Deborah Yeh, Kim Salem-Jackson, Crystal Files, Richard Dickson, Amy Thompson, Ciara Dilley, Jinder Bhogal, Jade Slater, Tim Diamond, Skye Healey Ward, Fiorella Campos, Elicia Azali, Carly

Kawaja, Mary Beth Laughton, Emily Thompson, Susan Thiele, Nancy Mohamed, Megan Edwards, Amanda Griffin, Karen Lane, Valerie Ivey, Megan Weiss, Kelly Hsu, Shannon Damen, Jenelle Sheridan, Johanna Guy, Sandra Stangl, Michelle Stagg, Bret Noveli, Aaron Rose, Julie Luker, Dava Huber, Natalie Barnum, Lauren Ginsberg, Irina Shandarivska, Lauren Flanigan, Marion Saenan, Steven Saenen, Justin Parnell, Mili Ladha, Danielle Fried, Sabrina Sierant, Olympia Portale, Jay Cooper, Rebecca Duke, Sally Barton, Lucia Barnechea, Maria Spaulding, Julia Rosenbloom, Mariama Boamah, Russ Cohn, Nicky Heckles, Jessica Weinstein, Julie Luker, Chris Bellinger, Isobel Futter, Sherry Polevoy, Amy Sharon, Anne-Lee Muck, Paula Blackmore-White, Elizabeth Staino, Jennifer Yomoah, Rich Rodriqguez-Mahal, Nathan Schuster, Kelsey Morgan, Coleen Cattell, Jenny Danzi, Linda Lagos, Beth Corso, Edith Bailey, Juliette Bosscher, Tonna Cunningham, Eric Graziano, and many more.

To our Purpose Coaches:

Tru Pettigrew, it's been an honor to take your work to the world, and we're deeply grateful for your presence in our lives.

Kirk Souder, we're blessed to have you in our lives; thanks for being a bringer of light!

BOBBY

Renee and Miles, you are the best part of my life. I love you always.

I owe my deepest gratitude to my family and friends, who have supported me throughout this journey. Mom, your unwavering love and belief in me have been my foundation. Lisa, you have always been my rock, and to all my aunts and uncles, your wisdom and guidance have been invaluable.

To my extended family, the moms who have nurtured me—Jan Cox, Mama Fair, Mama Mac, and Emma Holbrooke—thank you. To the men who raised and mentored me—Joe Nabinett, Dickie Cox, and Aaron Dean—your strength and support have been instrumental in shaping who I am.

My brothers—The Good Fellas, Shelby Ebanks, Eugene Uzoukwu, Juan Truesdale, Kenyan McDuffie, Mike Tucker, Silas Dobbins, Kirk Taylor, Stuart Roche, Jawhar Young, Omar Kashif, Akil Waite, Dao-Yi Chow, Kenny Mac, Tony Fair, Mike Riley, Eric Dawson, LeKeith Taylor, Andre Pinard, Chris Wade, Curtis House, Ouigi Theodore, Bobby Joseph, Jeff Mazzacano, Jason Mayden, Astor Chambers, Kenny Burns, Sabai Burnett, Damon Degraff, Donae Burston, Marcus Walton, and Ant Demby—you have been my pillars of strength, motivation, and support.

To the incredible women who inspire me—Nadia Laurinci, Bevy Smith, Kea Kirkland, Kelley Walton, Eunique Jones, Crystal Files, Cathy Hughes, Valencia Michell, Shannon Washington, Tauna Dean, Joy Davis Fair, Roxanne Leff, Sandra Blackburn, Tanya Deans, Julia Collins, Michaella Solar-March, Ruthie Schulder, Shani Langi, Sharice Belantonio, Sam Selolwane, and Sophie Ozoux—you show me what extraordinary looks like.

To the communities that have been my backbone—Direct Impulse, YARDstyle, AMPdi Crew, GoodFellas, Define New York Run Club, Morgan State University, Peace First, RIVET, The Brooklyn Circus, Brooklyn Kings, Good is the New Cool, and my speaking team, including Jasmine Them, Impact Eleven, Speakers Spotlight, and The Sweeney Agency—you have all been essential in my journey.

A special mention goes to the young people who bring joy and hope to my life. May this book remind you to live a life with Purpose: Sanai Uzoukwu, Kamryn Anthony, Arin Tucker, Michal Tucker, Nya Tucker, Jakara Jordan, Jaden Williams, Maya Chavis Sekai Ausar Poles, Christian Wright, Cameron Lewis, Tolulade Awodiya, Aniyah President, Charles Clarke Jr., Cole Fair, Reed Fair, Axel Miranda-Antonio, Aires Amor, Ava Leff, and Emory Leff, Casey and Michael Morsell.

Finally, to Bobby Lyles, a coach who saw my potential and Purpose and guided me with unwavering support and wisdom, thank you for transforming my life in ways I never imagined possible.

AFDHEL

With deep gratitude to:

My family: Rukshana and Nuri, you are my heart. My parents, for teaching me about moral courage and leadership.

My friends who make my life richer in so many ways: Leigh Walters-James, Brenton Smith, Ranidu Lankage, Paul Wool-mington, Ravin Fernando, Tasha Marikkar, Leah Marikkar, Penny Ferdinand, Piyumi Samaraweera, Romola Ratnam, Josie Naughton, Negar Tayyar, Shannon and Alex, Chris McConell, Janie McConnell, Meaghan Mihalic, Tom Spriggs, Jordan and Josselyn Delp, Francesca and Luciano, Maria and Antoine, Carla and Mauricio, David Rothenberg, Sharon and Coby Litvinsky, Paul Vu, Hayden Blaz, Greta Gamble, Tracy and Desh, Cindy and Rich, Chloe and Tom, Liz and Perry, Anna and Elliot, She-han and Kerry, Svante Lindeberg, Aushi and Eroshan, Raina and Jamie, Julian Bowyer, Nihal Arthanayake, Ruwanga Samath,

Dinesha Mendis, Deepa and David, Nicky Black, and my whole Sri Lanka crew.

My speaking crew: Jasmine Them, Amy Jean Sy, Martin and Farah Perlmuter and the whole Speakers Spotlight family, Marnie Ballane, Dwight Ireland, Kelli Thompson, Courtney Cooper, Alannah Ford, Paula Sage, Elise Bercovici-Diker, Tim Mathy, Rich Gibbons, Katie Bloomer, Farah Parkinson, Declan McManus, Daniel Hennes, Mike Gottesman, Mimi Hair, Dylan Kirkpatrick, Mandy Lubrano, Barrett Cordero, Debbie Barela. Amy Panchyshyn, Melanie Roy, Catherine McCabe, Zoila Solomon, Meredith Wilson, David Catchings, Melissa Narvaez, Mallory Ross, Sheridan Cooke, Annie Joshua, and so many others who have helped me speak around the world.

Purpose warriors who inspire me: Barb Groth, Cyril Gutsch, Deevee Kashi, Jessica Sibley, Lukas Derksen, Julia Collins, Kayalin Akens-Irby, Gwen Whiting, Maya Peterson, Fiona Korwin-Pawlowski, Farhoud Meybodi, Shani Langi, Sharice Belantonio, Chris Freel, Shannon de Laat, Bradon Peele, Christie Mann, Rachel Suckle, Sophie Ozoux, Kwame Taylor-Hayford, David Ohana, Tauna Dean, Chloe Franses, Zeppa Kreager, Jacob Cohen, Shiran Gort, Taras Kravtchouk, Kat Gordon, Chris Wade, Fanshen Cox, LeKeith Taylor, Omar Brownson, Justin Wilkenfeld, Jess Miller, Dana Snyder, Matt Pohlson, Carmen Lansdowne, Tim Coldwell, Tim Blair, David Constable, Philipp Haid, Sade Muhammad, Rachel Sumekh, Max Lenderman, Elyse Cohen, Ahmen, Nicolas Van Erum, Kelley Amadei, Masami Sato, Marco Vega, Noel Geer, Ant Demby, Elliot Kotek, Ian Schafer, Shaina Zafar, Luke Gledhill, Eternal Polk, Laura Rubin, Grant Trahant, Tom Herbst, Rebecca Nedelec, James Arthur Smith, Mark Brand, Andrea Serrano, Jon Vanhala, Jacki Spillane, Jennifer Solomon-Baum, Eric Raymond, Ajay Relan, Erik Wissa, David Trovato,

Lukas Mayrl, Tom Cartmale, Eric Liedtke, Timothy Nickloff, Andrew Hampp, Cruz Ortiz, Sanjay Sharma, Carolina Garcia-Jayaram, Vivek Jayaram, Adam Garone, Justin Dillon, Jen Hancock, Debra Cleaver, Casey Plasker, Adam Taubenfligel, Fernanda Romano, Anna Bulbrook, Michaella Solar-March, Wawa Gatheru, Rose Kentish, Jeff Scult, Todd Krim, Maya Penn, Lincoln Steffens, Daniel Flynn, Hank Fortener, David Hieatt, Aidaly Sosa, Eve Rodsky, Virginia Tenpenny, Vandana Hart, Grace Forrest, Marisa Hamamoto, Stepfanie Sword-Williams, Sascha Lewis, Amy Jo Martin, Ziad Ahamed, Ron Finley, Scott Harrison, Mark Rubinstein, Scott Budnick, Bob Deutsch, Rodney Franks, Sara Weinstein, Natalie Tran, Ruthie Schulder, Jessica Resler, Anna Bulbrook, Shaka Senghor, Jonathan Midenhall, Shaun Christie-David, Jacqueline Novogratz, Jennifer Silbert, Geena Rocero, Chalana Perera, Randhula de Silva, Galiano Tiramani, Olympia Auset, Frank Connelly, Gregory Constantin, Dr Lisa Dyson, Aurora James, Jai Al-Attas, Jameela Jamil, Lucia Chipoco, and everyone else around the world fighting to leave this world better than we found it.

Index